The Lost Ring
and other plays

Steve Fitzpatrick

CAMBRIDGE
UNIVERSITY PRESS

PUBLISHED BY THE PRESS SYNDICATE OF THE UNIVERSITY OF CAMBRIDGE
The Pitt Building, Trumpington Street, Cambridge CB2 1RP, United Kingdom

CAMBRIDGE UNIVERSITY PRESS
The Edinburgh Building, Cambridge CB2 2RU, United Kingdom
40 West 20th Street, New York, NY 10011–4211, USA
10 Stamford Road, Oakleigh, Melbourne 3166, Australia

First published 1985
Sixth printing 1997

Printed in the United Kingdom at the University Press, Cambridge

A catalogue record for this book is available from the British Library

ISBN 0 521 27895 3

Performance
These plays are protected by copyright. For permission to give a
public performance of any of the plays where an admission charge is
made, please write to Permissions Department, Cambridge
University Press, The Edinburgh Building, Shaftesbury Road,
Cambridge CB2 2RU.

Contents

STAGE DIRECTIONS

There are two kinds of direction in this playscript.
Those in **bold type** provide information that is
essential to an understanding of what is happening
in the play at that time. For a play-reading, these
should be read by a separate reader.

Those in *italic type* are less essential stage directions
and offer suggestions to assist with a production of
the play on stage. In a reading they are best not read
out as they will hamper the flow of the play,
although those who are reading may find that some
of these instructions offer help with the
interpretation of their lines.

The Lost Ring
A story from India

CHARACTERS

Male	Female
MADHAVA, the King's friend	SHAKUNTALA
KING DUSHYANTA	MANDARIKA
KANVA, the head of a hermitage	MALATI
SARADVATA, a suitor to Shakuntala	SERVANT-GIRL, in the palace
FISHERMAN	SINGER
1ST GUARD	FISHERMAN'S WIFE
2ND GUARD	MENAKA, mother of Shakuntala
	OLD WOMAN

(Enter Madhava.)

MADHAVA Hunting! - No-one but a fool or a king could enjoy hunting! We rise at the crack of dawn and go rushing about chasing deer and wild boar through the forest. In the heat of noon we go running after dangerous animals, getting scratched by thorns and bitten by flies. My legs are aching, I'm gasping for breath and I'm dying of thirst. And all because the King enjoys hunting!

(King Dushyanta enters, carrying a bow and arrows.)

KING Well, Madhava, we're certainly having excellent sport. I've never known such good hunting. Already we've found five tigers.

MADHAVA	When I go hunting I prefer to find as few tigers as possible. - It's all right for you. You're a warrior and a king. I'm an intellectual. I work with my brain.
KING	You? You're so lazy you've never read a book in your life.
MADHAVA	Perhaps not. But I think a lot. I have great thoughts.
KING	It's the first I've heard of it. What great thoughts have you had lately?
MADHAVA	I thought that instead of going hunting it would be much nicer to sit in the shade and relax. After all, don't the sages say that hunting is wrong, and that we mustn't kill?
KING	Not at all. Hunting is a noble sport. For generations the Kings of India have hunted in these forests. There's nothing to match the pleasures of the chase.
MADHAVA	Personally, I prefer chasing pretty girls. For one thing they're easier to catch, and for another -
KING	That will do. Don't forget, Madhava, that I'm your King as well as your friend. If you disapprove of hunting so much -
MADHAVA	Me? Disapprove of hunting? Whatever gave you that idea? Heaven forbid that I should disagree with my King.
KING	Then stop talking and follow me. - Look! There's a deer in the next clearing, gracefully swaying his neck as he grazes on the grass. I've never seen such a beautiful creature. Quick! Let's pursue him!

(The King goes off.)

MADHAVA   Well, that's all very well. But that deer won't look
so beautiful when he's hanging upside down from
a carrying-pole with the blood running from his
nostrils, will he? - Not that I've got anything
against hunting, of course. The way I look at it is -

> Whatever my opinions are
> Of this or that or other things,
> I fit my thoughts to suit my friends
> And never disagree with Kings.

(Madhava goes off after the King.)

**(Enter Shakuntala, with her friends Mandarika and
Malati.)**

SHAKUNTALA   Here, in this holy hermitage, far from the strife
and trouble of the world, we live in perfect peace.
And yet today I keep hearing birds in the forest
crying in alarm. What do you think could have
disturbed them?

MANDARIKA   Who knows? It's no concern of ours, after all.

MALATI   That's right, Shakuntala. Don't worry about the
birds. We've got to water the plants in this sacred
grove. That's what Kanva said before he went
away.

SHAKUNTALA   Yes, I know, Malati. It's our duty to obey Kanva,
the head of our community. - But all the same, I
wonder what alarmed the birds.

(Shakuntala mimes watering the plants.)

MANDARIKA   *(To Malati)* If you ask me, Shakuntala should be
pleased that Kanva's gone away.

MALATI   Why?

MANDARIKA   The rumour is he's gone to find a husband for her.

MALATI	Really?
MANDARIKA	So they say.
IAKUNTALA	What are you two giggling about?
MANDARIKA	Nothing.
MALATI	Mandarika says that Kanva's gone to get a husband for you.
IAKUNTALA	She's just saying what she wants for herself.
MANDARIKA	Well, what if I am? What's wrong with wanting a husband?
MALATI	Yes. If Kanva found *me* a husband, I'd take him.
IAKUNTALA	Wouldn't you want to see him for yourself first?
MALATI	Well, yes . . .
MANDARIKA	But that's all right. Kanva would never force you to marry someone you didn't like.
IAKUNTALA	Well, we shall see. - *(Looking off-stage)* What's that? - One of the deer belonging to the hermitage is running this way!
MANDARIKA	There's a hunter after him!
IAKUNTALA	Who could be so cruel as to hunt a harmless deer? - Quickly! Run and help him. I'll stay here and deal with the hunter.
	(Mandarika and Malati run off. The King enters from the other side.)
KING	Where is it? - Did you see a deer run by this way? Which way did it go?
IAKUNTALA	Put down your bow. You walk on sacred ground. - Why do you seek to kill your fellow-creatures and disturb the peace of this forest?

KING   *(Lowering his bow)* Forgive me. I was not aware I trod on holy ground. I was hunting in the forest and followed the deer to this place.

SHAKUNTALA   This is a holy hermitage, where those who've turned their backs upon the world live peacefully together. Here the deer have learned to trust mankind and lose their fear. Yet you, with your cruel arrows, take pleasure in their terror and their pain. Don't you know the bow you hold is to protect the weak, not hurt the innocent? Truly, hunting is a great evil.

KING   *(Aside)* How strange. She's angry with me, and I ought to be annoyed that she dares speak such harsh words to her King. And yet I do not mind at all. - *(To Shakuntala)* Forgive me. You are right. Hunting is cruel.

(Enter Madhava.)

MADHAVA   So there you are! - What happened to that deer?

KING   I let him go. - This is a sacred grove, Madhava, and this young woman says -

MADHAVA   Hello! A pretty girl! No wonder you let the deer get away.

KING   We were just discussing hunting -

MADHAVA   Hunting! Well, as you know, I agree with you about that. Hunting's a noble sport, there's nothing like it -

KING   On the contrary -

MADHAVA   Nothing can match the pleasures of the chase -

KING   Not at all.

MADHAVA   That's what you said -

KING   This young woman has reminded me that hunting is wrong and that we mustn't kill.

MADHAVA   But when I told you that five minutes ago you said I was talking nonsense!

KING   Madhava, why don't you go and see if that deer is hurt?

MADHAVA   I don't know where he is.

AKUNTALA   He's over there. See - my friends are tending to him.

MADHAVA   Ah! More girls! That's different then. You're right. I'd better go and see to that deer.

(Madhava goes off.)

AKUNTALA   You must forgive me, sir, if I was angry with you. I was forgetting the laws of hospitality.

KING   Not at all. You were right to be angry.

AKUNTALA   My name is Shakuntala. Allow me to welcome you to our hermitage.

KING   Thank you. But tell me, how does a young girl such as you come to dwell in this wilderness?

AKUNTALA   The story is a strange one. Perhaps you've heard of Kausika the hermit. He was my father.

KING   Yes, I've heard of him. He was famous for his penances and self-denial. He lived in the desert, eating and drinking as little as he could, and hardly seeing another human being. And as for women, he never went near one in his life. How can he be your father?

SHAKUNTALA   You're right. He was a man famous for his chastity, who made an oath never to touch a woman. But when the gods saw how a mere mortal could free himself from the desires of the body, they grew anxious, and Indra himself feared for his throne.

KING   Yes, I've heard that when a man can conquer all desire, even the gods are fearful of his power.

SHAKUNTALA   There is a nymph in heaven called Menaka, the most beautiful of all the immortals. Indra sent her to earth to tempt the strict hermit Kausika, and when he saw her he forgot his vows.

KING   That isn't strange. We often find a woman's beauty can be stronger than a warrior or a king.

SHAKUNTALA   So I have heard men say. As for what happened next –

KING   I understand.

SHAKUNTALA   It isn't hard to guess. At any rate, a child was born, and that child was me. My mother returned to heaven, my father went back to his penances and self-denial, and I was adopted by Kanva and brought up in this hermitage.

KING   If your mother had even half your beauty, I can understand how any hermit might forget his vows.

SHAKUNTALA   You mock me, sir.

KING   No, not for all the world. – But forgive me. You must have much to do. You have no time to waste talking to me.

SHAKUNTALA   No, I've plenty of time. – But of course, I mustn't keep you from your business.

KING   I've nothing to do. I'm waiting for my friend, Madhava, to catch up.

SHAKUNTALA   But you sent him on to tend to the deer.

KING   Yes. So I did. I'd forgotten. Then I suppose I'd better go and see what he's up to. - Which way did you say he went? - Ah, yes. I remember.

(The King goes off.)

SHAKUNTALA   How strange. He seemed confused, as if he had something more to say, yet didn't know what. Or do I think that just because I wanted to say more to him? What could I have to say to this stranger? - Nothing.

Yet even now, though he has gone away
And I remain alone,
My thoughts fly after him, as if they were
His thoughts and not my own.

(Shakuntala goes off.)

(Enter Madhava.)

MADHAVA   It's always the same. If it isn't one thing it's another. One day the King is bursting with energy and wanting to rush about killing animals, and the next he's mooning about like a half-wit and isn't interested in doing anything at all. I don't know what's the matter with him. He couldn't even eat his dinner! And when a man isn't interested in food there's something seriously wrong.

(Enter the King.)

MADHAVA
continued
Here he comes now. I'll see if I can cheer him up. - *(To the King)* So there you are! Isn't it a beautiful day? Why don't you go out in the forest and hunt animals?

KING
I've told you, Madhava, I've seen the error of my ways. I no longer enjoy hunting.

MADHAVA
Then you should be glad that you've come to your senses at last. Now we can go back to the palace and stop living like savages.

KING
I can't return to the palace. I must stay here.

MADHAVA
What do you want to stay here for? - People talk about the peace and quiet of the country, but give me the noisy comfort of the town any day.

KING
I can't leave this place.

MADHAVA
Why ever not?

KING
Madhava, you remember the beautiful girl we met yesterday?

MADHAVA
Which one? There are so many pretty girls it's hard to keep track of them all.

KING
Which one? The one whose beauty surpasses all others and dims the sun and moon, of course!

MADHAVA
I don't remember anyone like that.

KING
Of course you do! How could anyone forget her?

MADHAVA
My mind's gone blank.

KING
The girl at the hermitage, called Shakuntala. You must remember her.

MADHAVA
Oh, her!

KING
I've never seen anyone so beautiful in my life.

MADHAVA
Oh, so that's it!

KING   What?

MADHAVA   That's why you're wandering about like a man lost in a dream. You're in love.

KING   In love?

MADHAVA   Fortunately, I know the cure for that. What you need is a change of scene. Back in the city I'll show you so many pretty girls you'll forget about her in no time.

KING   I don't want to forget her! - Besides, it's impossible I ever could. I've got to see her again.

MADHAVA   Well, that's easy enough. You're the King, aren't you? You can do what you like.

KING   But she's led a sheltered life here in the hermitage. Perhaps she's even taken a vow never to marry.

MADHAVA   I thought you just wanted to see her, not to marry her.

KING   I don't know what I want. All I know is that I've got to see her.

MADHAVA   Well, she's not invisible, is she? Go and see her.

KING   But what can I say to her?

MADHAVA   I'm sure you'll think of something. Tell her you want to apologise for hunting that poor deer yesterday. Or if all else fails, tell her the truth.

KING   Yes, you're right. I'll go and see her at once.

(The King goes off.)

MADHAVA   I don't know. Why do people make such a fuss about something as common as falling in love? Especially if it just makes them miserable when they do. If you don't enjoy it, then why do it?

> I fall in love three times a week,
> But if it caused me pain
> I'd much prefer I never saw
> A pretty girl again.

(Madhava goes off after the King.)

(Enter Shakuntala, Mandarika and Malati.)

MANDARIKA   But, Shakuntala, won't you tell us what's the matter?

SHAKUNTALA   Nothing's the matter.

MALATI   Yes, there is. You're not yourself. What's wrong?

SHAKUNTALA   It's just the heat.

MANDARIKA   *(To Malati)* She's been like this since yesterday. Ever since that stranger visited us.

SHAKUNTALA   That was when the heat started to get so unbearable.

MANDARIKA   Not at all. It's much cooler today.

MALATI   Can't you feel the breeze?

SHAKUNTALA   You're mistaken. The heat is much worse.

MANDARIKA   *(To Malati)* You know, if I didn't know better, I'd say she was in love.

SHAKUNTALA   Nonsense!

MALATI   Yes, she's behaving just like people do in books when they fall in love.

SHAKUNTALA   I won't listen to such foolishness. I'll leave you. I'm not fit for any company except my own.

(Shakuntala goes off.)

MALATI   Yes, she's exactly like the people in the books.

MANDARIKA   But who can she be in love with?

MALATI   Not many people visit us. There was that hunter yesterday -

(Enter the King.)

And here he is again. - Welcome, sir.

KING   Thank you. Where's your friend today?

MANDARIKA   She's just this moment left us. She's not well.

KING   What? Is she ill? What's wrong with her?

MALATI   We think that she's in love.

KING   In love?

MALATI   Judging from the people in the books.

KING   Who with?

MALATI   She didn't say.

KING   Where is she?

MANDARIKA   Over there.

(The King goes off after Shakuntala.)

MALATI   He's gone.

MANDARIKA   How strange. You don't suppose -

(Enter Madhava.)

MADHAVA   Hello. It's me again. Have you seen the King?

MALATI }
MANDARIKA } *(Together)* The King?

MADHAVA   Didn't you know he was the King?

MALATI   How could we know? He didn't say.

MADHAVA   He must have forgotten to mention it. He was coming to visit your friend.

MANDARIKA   Yes, he was here just now. He was behaving rather oddly.

MADHAVA   That's because he's in love.

MANDARIKA   In love?

MALATI   That's strange. We think Shakuntala's in love as well.

MADHAVA   Now there's a coincidence.

MALATI   Do you think they could be in love with each other?

MADHAVA   I wouldn't be surprised. Where is he?

MANDARIKA   He went to find her.

MADHAVA   Then thank the gods for that. Soon it'll all be settled and we'll be able to relax.

MALATI   Will he ask her to marry him?

MADHAVA   He might. Love makes a man do all sorts of strange things.

MALATI   The books all say love is a powerful god who can make us do what he likes.

MADHAVA   That's true. He plays with us like a spoilt child with his toys. Love makes us suffer and rejoice, imprisons us and sets us free, makes us more noble than we are and makes us do all sorts of silly things. If it wasn't the only thing which makes life worth living we'd be much better off without it.

MALATI   The books all say that love brings perfect happiness and joy.

MADHAVA   You don't want to believe the things you read in books. Love brings all sorts of things. You can't rely on it at all.

MANDARIKA   But, all the same, everybody wants to fall in love.

MADHAVA   That's because they don't realise what hard work it is. Personally, I'm not prepared to take it on. I'm too lazy. There are so many girls in the world I'd never have the energy to decide which one I liked the best.

MALATI   Do you think love will bring happiness to Shakuntala and the King?

MADHAVA   Who can say? *(Looking off-stage)* Here they come now.

MANDARIKA   We'd best withdraw, and leave them to themselves.

MADHAVA   By all means. People in love are never very interesting company.

(Madhava, Mandarika and Malati go off. Shakuntala and the King enter from the other side.)

KING   You know I love you, and you say you love me too. So it's obvious. We must get married at once.

SHAKUNTALA   You know my heart, and since you are the King it's lawful for us to marry without my guardian's consent. But wouldn't it be better to wait till Kanva returns?

KING   How can you make me wait? You belong to no-one but yourself. You alone can give yourself to me. We have only to make our faithful promises to each other and we are man and wife.

SHAKUNTALA   Forgive me. I know little of the world, yet I have often heard that men deceive women, and their promises can't be trusted. I cannot think that you would treat me so, and yet I'm still afraid.

KING   It's true that many men do break their promises and deny their love - and so do women too, for all of us are weak. But when we see beauty such as yours it makes us better than we know. How could I break my word to you? You needn't be afraid.

SHAKUNTALA   You know I must believe you.

KING   *(Putting a ring on her finger)*
        Then take this ring, and wear it for my sake -
        A token of my love,
        To seal the solemn promise that I swear
        By all the gods above.

(The King and Shakuntala go off.)

(Enter Mandarika.)

MANDARIKA   *(To audience)* Two months have passed. The King stayed for as long as he could, but duties of state called him back to the palace a month ago. Shakuntala stayed behind till Kanva returned. But now that he's come home she leaves today to join the King in the capital. - But I was right that Kanva went away to find a husband for her. He's brought a powerful sage called Saradvata home with him, and there'll be trouble when Saradvata finds out that she's already married and is expecting the King's child. - I'm going to keep out of the way.

(Mandarika goes off, as Kanva and Saradvata enter from the other side.)

SARADVATA   Married? You tell me she is married?

KANVA   Yes, Saradvata, I'm afraid she is. I told you she
           was free to make her own decision, and while I
           was away visiting you it seems she's made it.

SARADVATA It isn't possible. How could she marry without
           your consent?

KANVA   She met a hunter who turned out to be the King,
           and kings, you know, marry by just exchanging
           promises. The law doesn't require a guardian's
           consent for them.

SARADVATA Have you met this king?

KANVA   No. He had to return to the capital.

SARADVATA I thought as much. It's just a trick. This king is
           nothing but a figment of her imagination.

KANVA   He gave Shakuntala a ring to seal his vow. I've
           seen it - a ring with the royal seal - I'm afraid
           you've had a wasted journey. I'm sorry.

SARADVATA It can't be true.

KANVA   She's already with child by him. I'm sorry if
           you're disappointed -

SARADVATA Then I'm rejected? I, who have studied the classic
           writings and the books of ancient secrets, am
           rejected as if I were of no account!

KANVA   I'm sorry. I know you love Shakuntala, but I
           made no promises -

SARADVATA Now I see that women's eyes are quickly drawn
           from true virtue by the pomp and power of kings.
           She's rejected me - a man famed for learning and
           good works - and given herself to a man with
           nothing noble about him but his crown.

KANVA   I'm sorry that you feel this way. I know you love her, but there's nothing I can do. - Now, if you'll excuse me, I must go and prepare for her departure.

(Kanva goes off.)

SARADVATA   No. I don't love her. I won't love a woman who rejects me. If I can't possess her beauty it is nothing but a poison to me. - But I will be revenged. This king may think he's set his claim upon her with his ring around her finger, but a king's power is as nothing to the power of one skilled in the ancient wisdom. I'll put a curse upon them. - She will lose that ring, that token of his love, and while the ring is lost the King will lose all memory of ever meeting her. She'll vanish from his mind, and be rejected just as she rejected me. And never, till the ring is found, will he remember her. Then they will feel the misery that I feel now, and justice will be done.

(Saradvata goes off. From the other side Kanva, Shakuntala, Mandarika and Malati enter.)

KANVA   Come on, Shakuntala, it's time for you to leave.

SHAKUNTALA   I long to see my husband, yet I'm sad to have to leave my home.

MALATI   Your home is with your husband now.

MANDARIKA   You'll soon forget about us when you're Queen.

SHAKUNTALA   I'll never forget my friends, or the happy days I've spent here.

KANVA   You've been more than a daughter to me, but I part from you with joy, knowing you'll be the best of wives. Go to the King whose ring you wear and make him happy.

ЇAKUNTALA	*(Looking at her hand)* The ring! Where is it? It's gone!
ЇANDARIKA	What? Have you lost it?
ЇAKUNTALA	Where can it be?
MALATI	When did you see it last?
ЇAKUNTALA	I had it when I went to bathe.
ЇANDARIKA	You must have lost it in the river!
ЇAKUNTALA	What shall I do?
KANVA	Don't worry. If the ring is lost it can't be helped. The King has many more jewels in his treasure house.
ЇAKUNTALA	But it was a token of his love.
KANVA	His love, I'm sure, is not so easily lost as a ring. It's time to go. Your husband waits for you To come and be his wife. Now reap the harvest of your ripened love And live a happy life.

(Kanva embraces Shakuntala, and she goes off one way, while Kanva, Mandarika and Malati go off the other.)

(Enter Madhava and a servant-girl, from opposite sides of the stage.)

MADHAVA	Hello! A pretty girl! – I haven't seen you before. When did you come to the palace?
ЇRVANT-GIRL	I've been a servant here a month and more, but you've been away on your hunting trip with the King, so you wouldn't have seen me.
MADHAVA	No, it took longer than we thought. The King found more than he bargained for in the forest.

SERVANT-GIRL   What do you mean?

MADHAVA   I don't think I'm supposed to tell anyone. The King hasn't said a word about it since we returned, and since he couldn't talk about anything else before I think he must want to keep it a secret.

SERVANT-GIRL   Keep what a secret?

MADHAVA   That's what I'm not supposed to tell you. You'll find out soon enough. He'll tell you himself in his own good time.

SERVANT-GIRL   Do you know where the King is? There's someone at the gate who wants to see him.

MADHAVA   I'll find him for you. He can't be far away.

(**Madhava goes off. Immediately, the King enters from the other side, attended by servants, musicians etc.**)

KING   Come! Let me have some music! - Sing that song again, the one about the woman yearning for her departed lover.

SINGER   Yes, my lord.

KING   It's strange I find that song so moving, for I'm not separated from any loved one. It must be that when we hear sweet music it recalls the sorrows we felt in a former life.

SERVANT-GIRL   My lord, there is someone to see you at the gate, a girl from a hermitage. Shall I admit her now, or wait until you've heard the song?

KING   Let her come in. It's a King's duty to welcome strangers.

(The servant-girl goes off.)

What business can a girl from a hermitage have with me? - Well, we will soon find out.

(The servant-girl re-enters with Shakuntala.)

RVANT-GIRL Here is your visitor, my lord.

KING Yes? What have you to say to me?

IAKUNTALA My lord, my tongue can't find the words to say what joy it is to see you.

KING But what can I do for you?

IAKUNTALA Why, nothing. It's enough for me to be with you.

KING Nothing? Then why have you come to see me?

IAKUNTALA What do you mean, my lord?

KING If you've some business with me, then say what it is.

IAKUNTALA My lord, why is your tone so cold? Have I offended you?

KING Offended me? No. But say what it is you want.

IAKUNTALA I've come to be with my husband.

KING Your husband? Why, where is he?

IAKUNTALA Is this a joke?

KING Come, come, don't try my patience. State your business or depart.

IAKUNTALA Is this the way to welcome back your wife?

KING My wife?

IAKUNTALA You frighten me.

KING What are you saying? You, my wife? - I've never seen you before in my life.

SHAKUNTALA	My lord, you married me and swore to be a faithful husband.
KING	The woman is mad!
SHAKUNTALA	Do you deny it?
KING	I swear by all the gods I've never set eyes on you before.
SHAKUNTALA	Don't you recognise me?
KING	How could I? - Either you're mad, or you've some evil reason for telling these lies. I've heard enough. - Depart!
SHAKUNTALA	Then there's no faith or honesty in all the world, if you deny me. I trusted you and gave myself freely, without my guardian's consent, with no witnesses, believing your promises and taking lies for truth. If you no longer love me, or you never loved me, that is misery enough. But I would rather suffer that than bear the shame of such deceit as yours. To act as you have done would be dishonourable in the meanest beggar. Are you, a King, not ashamed to face me with such lies?
KING	I refuse to listen to these insults. I don't know you. Leave my sight.
SHAKUNTALA	If you reject me, will you deny your child as well? In me you turn away your own flesh and blood, for I bear your child.
KING	So you are pregnant too. Your own words prove you are no better than a whore.
SHAKUNTALA	I am your lawful wife!
KING	If I'd married you, I'd have given you some token of my love. Show me that if you want me to believe you.

AKUNTALA   My lord, you gave me a ring to seal your promise, but I have lost it –

KING   How very convenient! – The woman is obviously lying. Take her away.

AKUNTALA   Hear me, my lord. You think that no-one sees your evil, but the gods see and will punish you. You think that as a King you are above the law, but the law is above us all, and knows what is in our hearts. You are yourself a witness to the truth you swore to me, and to the lies that you tell now. If you break your word you're nothing but a thief stealing your own honour, a traitor conspiring against your own crown. If you have no charity towards me, then have mercy on yourself. Don't do yourself this wrong.

KING   My conscience is clear. I've done nothing wrong. Why should anyone believe your word against that of a King?

AKUNTALA   My lord, a woman carries a child for nine months, nourishing it within her, and gives birth in pain. Thus, through his wife a man is born again, and from her receives sons and daughters to bring him joy. Through his children a man lives on after he is dead. Whatever I have done to lose your love, don't reject your child and cast away your other self. Even the cruel tiger cares for his young and is tender with his children. The smallest bird will fight a snake to protect his young ones in the nest.

KING   Enough of this! It's well known that women are liars. Anyone can see you're just a whore trying to find a father for her bastard. – Take her away.

SHAKUNTALA   The evil see nothing but evil in others, yet their own evil they cannot see. - Perhaps you think you can treat me this way because I am a woman. But beware. Though I am weak now and you are strong, it will not always be so. Remember that on this earth nothing can last for ever. The time will come when you are miserable and alone, as I am now, begging for kindness and a friendly word. On that day I pray that you will find a heart as cold and hard as stone, as yours has been to me. - Now I will trouble you no more. Farewell.

(Shakuntala goes off. A pause.)

KING   Make sure that madwoman is never admitted to my presence again. - Now. Let's forget her. We were going to hear a song. Come. I'll hear it out on the terrace.

SINGER   Yes, my lord.

KING   It's strange. -
I feel some sorrow weighing on my mind,
And yet I don't know what -
As if my heart were troubled by some pain
I long ago forgot.

(All go off.)

(Enter a fisherman, carrying a huge fish, and his wife, from opposite sides of the stage.)

FISHERMAN   Wife! Wife! Wonderful news! I've caught the biggest fish you've ever seen in your life.

WIFE   Where on earth did you find that? I've never seen such a fish.

FISHERMAN   Nor me.

WIFE   What are you going to do with it?

FISHERMAN   I don't know.

WIFE   You should take it to the King.

FISHERMAN   The King?

WIFE   A fish like that. He'll have it for his dinner.

FISHERMAN   Yes, you're right. It's a fish fit for a King. He'll give us a great reward for a fish like this.

WIFE   It must be our lucky day!

FISHERMAN   Give me the knife so that I can gut it. Then we'll take it to the King.

WIFE   *(Giving him a knife)* Here you are.

(The fisherman slices the fish's belly open to remove its guts.)

FISHERMAN   That's strange. What's this?

WIFE   What is it?

FISHERMAN   It's a ring. *(He takes it out.)* A gold ring set with diamonds.

WIFE   What's it doing inside a fish?

FISHERMAN   He must have swallowed it.

WIFE   A ring like that must be worth a fortune.

FISHERMAN   At least! This really is our lucky day. We'll take the fish to the King, and sell the ring in the market.

WIFE   We'll be rich!

FISHERMAN   Then come along. Good fortune waits for us.
Come on - Don't dawdle, wife -
Let's reap the harvest of this lucky day
And live a happy life.

(They go off with the fish.)

(Enter two palace-guards, from opposite sides of the stage.)

1ST GUARD	Anything to report?
2ND GUARD	No, sir. All quiet.
1ST GUARD	No sign of that madwoman the King ordered us to keep away from him?
2ND GUARD	No. If you ask me, he's seen the last of her.
1ST GUARD	Good.

(Enter the fisherman and his wife.)

	Who's this? - What do you want?
FISHERMAN	We've come with a gift for the King.
1ST GUARD	What sort of gift?
WIFE	A fish.
1ST GUARD	A fish?
FISHERMAN	And what a fish! It's the biggest I've ever seen.
WIFE	It's for the King's dinner.
1ST GUARD	I see. - *(To the 2nd guard)* Go and see if the King wants a fish for his dinner.
2ND GUARD	Yes, sir.

(He goes off.)

WIFE	Do you think the King will give us a great reward?
1ST GUARD	He may do. You never know with kings.
FISHERMAN	Even if he doesn't, we've still got the ring.
1ST GUARD	Ring? What ring?

FISHERMAN   *(Showing him the ring)* This.

1ST GUARD   *(Examining the ring)* This ring bears the King's seal. Where did you get it?

FISHERMAN   I found it in the belly of the fish.

1ST GUARD   In the fish? A likely tale! You stole it!

WIFE   No, we found it in the fish.

1ST GUARD   You stole it, you thieves! You're under arrest.

FISHERMAN   But it was in the fish, I swear it!

1ST GUARD   How could the King's ring get in a fish?

FISHERMAN   I don't know. He must have lost it somehow and the fish swallowed it.

WIFE   Yes, that's right.

1ST GUARD   Then why hasn't he said anything about it? Do you think the King could lose a valuable ring like this and just forget about it?

(Enter King and 2nd guard.)

KING   What's this I hear about a fish? Where are the kind people who've brought me this gift?

1ST GUARD   Here, my lord. They're under arrest.

KING   Under arrest? What for?

1ST GUARD   They've got a ring belonging to you. They claim they found it.

KING   I haven't lost a ring.

1ST GUARD   That's what I thought. They must have stolen it.

FISHERMAN   We didn't, my lord! We found it in the belly of the fish.

1ST GUARD   A likely story!

KING   Let me see the ring.

1ST GUARD   *(Giving him the ring)* Here, my lord.

(The King looks at the ring. A long pause.)

What's the matter, my lord? You've turned pale. - *(To the fisherman and his wife)* You see? The King is angry with you. Look how pale he is.

FISHERMAN   We're done for!

1ST GUARD   *(To the King)* Shall I take these thieves away to prison, my lord?

KING   No. Set them free. And reward them well.

WIFE   We're saved!

KING   I did lose this ring.

1ST GUARD   You did?

KING   At least, I gave it to somebody who lost it.

1ST GUARD   You mean their story's true?

KING   A great cloud is lifted from my mind. And I remember now what I have thrown away.

1ST GUARD   What do you mean, my lord?

KING   No matter. Reward these people well. Give them five hundred pieces of gold.

FISHERMAN   Thank you, my lord.

WIFE   May the gods bless you!

KING   I've thrown away the blessings of the gods. Nothing is left for me but misery.

(The King goes off.)

2ND GUARD   What's the matter with him?

1ST GUARD	Who knows? - *(To fisherman and wife)* But you two have had a lucky escape.
FISHERMAN	Five hundred pieces of gold!
WIFE	We're rich!
FISHERMAN	*(To guards)* You must come and drink with us to celebrate.
1ST GUARD	Now you're talking!
WIFE	What about the fish?
FISHERMAN	We'll eat it ourselves! Come on! - There'll be rejoicing in our house tonight - Good luck is here to stay! And everyone must help us celebrate This joyful, happy day!

(They go off.)

(Enter Madhava and the servant-girl.)

MADHAVA	I've never seen anyone so miserable.
SERVANT-GIRL	Ever since he found that ring and remembered he really did marry Shakuntala he's been plunged in despair.
MADHAVA	He doesn't sleep at night, he's not interested in hunting or music, he hardly touches his food. He's in a terrible state. - It's all his own fault, of course. If he loves the girl so much why on earth did he send her away?
SERVANT-GIRL	He says he forgot about her.
MADHAVA	How can you forget about someone you've just married? If you ask me he had it all planned. He regretted marrying her, and meant to deny her. That's why he kept quiet about it after we came

home. Frankly I'm shocked. If you make a promise you should keep it. - And now he's sorry that he treated her so badly. Well, it serves him right.

SERVANT-GIRL   Sssh! He's coming.

(Enter the King.)

MADHAVA   He looks worse than ever. I'll try to cheer him up. - *(To King)* How are you today? Why don't you listen to your musicians, or go out in the gardens and enjoy the flowers? Or you could go hunting. There are so many pleasures it's hard to know which to choose.

KING   Sorry, Madhava, did you say something?

MADHAVA   Here I am, trying to cheer you up, and you don't even listen.

KING   I'm sorry. But you're wasting your time. I can never be happy again. I've lost my reason for living.

MADHAVA   You threw it away, you mean. It's all your own fault. What did you want to go and send her away for?

KING   You're right to reproach me. I deserve all you can say and more.

MADHAVA   Well, since you mention it, yes, you do. You know I'd never say a word against my King, but it was wrong to marry that poor girl and gain her trust, and then deny her and send her away like that.

KING   I know, Madhava. Yet my mind was clouded by some strange power and my memory of her slept until I saw the ring. But I am punished for my cruelty to her.

MADHAVA	Well, at least you're sorry for it now.
KING	I could bear my own misery at losing her. But when I think of her despair when I sent her away, and I remember her words to me, and when I think of her wandering alone, hopeless, rejected by her husband, then my pain is greater than I can bear.
ERVANT-GIRL	Is there nothing you can do to find her, my lord?
KING	I've sent to the hermitage, but she didn't return there. No-one has seen her since the day I sent her away. Perhaps in despair she took her own life, or starved in the desert. All hope of seeing her again is gone.
ERVANT-GIRL	Don't say that. Why, the way you found the ring again shows that anything can happen and that we should never despair.
MADHAVA	That's true. If you can find your ring in the belly of a fish you must have the gods on your side.
KING	But even if I were to find her again she'd hate me for what I did to her, and rightly too.
ERVANT-GIRL	If she loves you she'll forgive you.
KING	No, she'll reject me as I once rejected her. That's all I deserve. Even if she could forgive the way I treated her, how could she forgive the way I denied our unborn child? I was a tyrant when I sent her away, but only a monster would reject his child.
ERVANT-GIRL	Why do you torment yourself like this? You wrong your wife again in thinking she couldn't forgive you. While you remain apart neither of you can be happy. Go and search for her.

KING   But where shall I look?

SERVANT-GIRL   My lord, trust in the gods. What more can any of us do?

KING   Well, I will go. But not in hopes of finding her, but only to relieve my misery by labouring on her behalf.

MADHAVA   Then I'll come with you.

KING   No. I must go alone, without a friend or servant or any of the privileges of royalty, and live the life of an outcast from the world.
Fortune was kind, but I refused her gifts,
And now her wheel is turned.
So I must go and bear without complaint
The sorrow I have earned.

(The King, Madhava and the servant-girl go off.)

(Enter Menaka.)

MENAKA   I am the nymph Menaka, the mother of Shakuntala. From heaven I have watched my daughter's suffering under the curse of the lost ring. And I have seen the King, her husband, driven by remorse and grief, set out in search of her. Since then many months have passed. Shakuntala and her child are safe. I guided her to a distant hermitage, high in the mountains, and there she was safely delivered of a son. As for the King, he wandered from village to village, through forests and over hills, and across the waterless plains. The sun beat down upon his head, and the wind blew dust in his eyes. Hunger and thirst were his companions on the road, and when the rainy season came his clothes rotted upon his back. At the outskirts of the villages the children threw stones at him, and the dogs stopped scratching their fleas to chase him away. And still he travelled on.

(Enter the King dressed in rags.) *(Menaka retires to watch the action.)*

KING   The world has more to hurt us than I ever knew. When, as a King, I used to see the beggars at my gate I pitied them, and yet I never knew what I should pity them for. Once I was proud of all the charity I gave the weak and poor, but in my weakness and my poverty I see that charity is no excuse for pride. I have been beaten, hungry, threatened and abused, and yet I live no worse than many of my subjects, and much better than the animals of the forest like the harmless deer I used to hunt. - Now I like to watch the gentle deer, and feed them when I can, for they remind me of Shakuntala, my wife. When I remember her the only grief I feel is for her sorrow now. My own unhappiness I've put behind me, for I don't deserve to have her for my wife. Now when I think of her I remember only the happiness we knew so briefly, and I forget my hunger and my weariness.

(Enter an old woman, carrying a baby.)

OLD WOMAN   Who are you, stranger? What are you doing here?

KING   I am a traveller. I'll do you no harm. What place is this?

OLD WOMAN   This is a hermitage, where holy men pray for this wicked world.

KING   I visited a hermitage once - but no matter. Is that your child you hold?

OLD WOMAN   Mine? I'm too old to be the mother of a baby. My children all have children of their own. I'm just his nurse. His mother lives at the hermitage.

KING   He's a pretty child.

OLD WOMAN   He takes after his mother in that.

KING   May I hold him?

OLD WOMAN   Hold him? What kind of man are you? It's woman's work, tending to children. Besides, I don't know who you are. You don't look like a man that can be trusted.

KING   Forgive me, I've no children of my own, so when I see another's child I feel more tenderness than another man.

OLD WOMAN   That's all very well, but I can't let this child be touched by any filthy beggar that happens to pass by.

KING   No, of course not. I'm sorry. Who is the child's father? Is he a hermit too?

OLD WOMAN   Don't mention that man to me.

KING   Why not?

OLD WOMAN   A vile, deceiving monster who rejected his own lawful wife!

KING   What?

OLD WOMAN   A lying villain, even if he is a king!

KING   What are you saying?

(Enter Shakuntala.)

O, gods! What do I see?

SHAKUNTALA *(To the old woman)* I'll take the child now, before he grows troublesome. - *(She notices the King.)* But who is this? Why do you stare at me that way? Your face reminds me of one I used to know, and yet your clothes mark you as a wandering beggar. Who are you, sir?

KING *(Kneeling)* O, Shakuntala, my face is changed. Hunger and sorrow have left their marks on me. I am a man unworthy of your regard. Yet I have something that belongs to you which I must return. You lost this ring. Take it again and wear it or throw it away, for it is yours to do with as you will.

(He gives her the ring. A long pause.)

SHAKUNTALA Rise up, my lord. You must not kneel to me. You are my husband and my King.

OLD WOMAN What's this? You are her husband?

KING That is a name I have no right to any more. - But do you remember the words you spoke to me? - 'The time will come when you are miserable and alone, begging for kindness and a friendly word. On that day I pray that you will find a heart as cold and hard as stone, as yours has been to me.' - That day has come. Take your revenge, and may it be as sweet as all the grief I caused was bitter.

SHAKUNTALA *(Kneeling)* My lord, please don't remind me of the foolish words I spoke in anger. I am your faithful wife. If you love me once again then all my sorrow was nothing but a dream, forgotten as soon as we awake.

KING Can you forgive me?

SHAKUNTALA Take the child, my lord, and look upon your son.

(The old woman gives the baby to the King. Menaka comes forward.)

MENAKA   My daughter, my son. I have watched the progress of your sorrows from above, and I have guided your ways to meet again. You suffered under the curse of one disappointed in love, yet do not blame him, for the power of love is as great for evil as it is for good. Only rejoice that you are reunited, and that the ring, so easily lost, was found again.

For lovers, as you know, are often weak,
But love itself is strong.
Though, like a ring, love may be quickly lost
It will endure as long.

The Stupid Judge
Stories from Russia and elsewhere

CHARACTERS

ELENA THE WISE
OLD WOMAN
RICH BROTHER
POOR BROTHER
WOOD-CUTTER
THE WOOD-CUTTER'S WIFE
A MERCHANT'S WIDOW
SHEMIAKA, the stupid Judge
OFFICER OF THE COURT
IDIOT
GUARDS
FARMER'S WIFE
PRIEST
DOCTOR
MAID-SERVANT
A WOMAN WHO LENT MONEY
A MAN WHO BORROWED MONEY

The open-air court of Shemiaka the Judge. There is a chair for the Judge, and various other benches and chairs.

(The Old Woman is sweeping the floor. Enter Elena the Wise.)

ELENA   Is this the court of Shemiaka the Judge?

OLD WOMAN   It is. And who might you be?

ELENA   People call me Elena the Wise.

OLD WOMAN   Indeed? I've heard of you. Well, we could do with some wisdom around here. There doesn't seem to be enough of it to go round.

ELENA   It's the same everywhere. I do my best, but I can't be everywhere at once. What sort of a judge have you got here?

OLD WOMAN   Shemiaka? Between you and me, he's the most stupid judge in the whole of Russia. Which is saying something. - Still, it's none of my business. I just keep the place clean.

ELENA   But can't anything be done about him?

OLD WOMAN   Not really. He's the Judge, after all. Call him an idiot - which would be putting it mildly - and he'd send you to prison.

ELENA   But don't people complain?

OLD WOMAN   All the time.

               (Enter the Rich Brother, leading the Poor Brother who is tied up with rope, the Wood-Cutter, the Wood-Cutter's Wife, and the Merchant's Widow.)

RICH BROTHER   Judge Shemiaka! - Why does it have to be him?

WOOD-CUTTER   Everyone knows he's a fool.

WIDOW   He's the biggest idiot for miles around.

RICH BROTHER   With an ordinary judge you know where you are. You pay him a bribe, and provided the other side doesn't pay him a bigger bribe he decides in your favour. That's what justice means. But with this fellow you never know what he might do.

OLD WOMAN   Are you bringing a case for Shemiaka to judge?

CH BROTHER	It's perfectly straightforward. *(Pointing to Poor Brother)* This man mutilated my horse.
WIFE	He killed my baby!
WIDOW	He murdered my husband!
CH BROTHER	It's an open-and-shut case. Nobody could mess it up.
OLD WOMAN	Shemiaka will manage.
CH BROTHER	We'll just have to pay him a bigger bribe and hope for the best.
	(Enter Shemiaka at the back of the stage, unseen by the others.)
OOD-CUTTER	It's disgraceful! Somebody ought to do something about such idiots.
WIFE	He's a public laughing-stock. Everyone knows he's a fool.
WIDOW	My dear departed husband always said he was a complete imbecile.
CH BROTHER	He's the most thick-witted, feeble-minded, brainless drivelling dunce to ever walk this earth.
SHEMIAKA	Good morning, good people. What can I do for you?
CH BROTHER	Ah, good morning, your Honour. We were just talking about you.
	(Pause.)
SHEMIAKA	About me?
CH BROTHER	*(After another pause)* And then we got on to talking about all these fools and idiots one meets around the place nowadays - people not like you at all - I'm sure you've come across them. Absolutely disgraceful.

SHEMIAKA   Oh, yes. Terrible.

RICH BROTHER We were just saying that a man like you - a man
              of wisdom and intelligence - is exactly what's
              needed to deal with these idiots.

WOOD-CUTTER   That's right.

WIDOW   Absolutely.

SHEMIAKA   It's funny you should say that. Everywhere I go,
              I'm always hearing people complaining about
              stupidity. There's far too much of it about.

RICH BROTHER Exactly.

SHEMIAKA   It's my duty as a judge to do something about it.
              The trouble is I never seem to meet any idiots
              myself. It's always other people. - But something
              must be done! Where's the Officer of the Court?

OLD WOMAN   He's still having breakfast. - *(Calling)* Ivan! The
              Judge wants you.

              **(The Officer of the Court enters hurriedly, doing up
              the buttons of his uniform.)**

OFFICER   I'm coming, I'm coming! - Sorry, your Honour, I
              was just attending to some important court
              business -

SHEMIAKA   I want you to take some of your men, and go and
              arrest all the idiots in town.

OFFICER   Arrest all the idiots?

SHEMIAKA   That's right.

OFFICER   What for?

SHEMIAKA   For being idiots, of course. What do you think?

OFFICER   Oh . . . yes. Where will I find them?

SHEMIAKA	How should I know? That's your job.
OFFICER	Yes, but –
SHEMIAKA	No excuses! Go and arrest an idiot at once, or I'll have you arrested.
OFFICER	Yes, but –
SHEMIAKA	At once!
OFFICER	Yes, your Honour. **(He goes off.)**
SHEMIAKA	That's the way to do things. Be firm. Too many judges are content to sit back and do nothing about the problem of idiots in our society. But I take my responsibilities more seriously. Now, what can I do for you?
CH BROTHER	Well, first of all we wanted to offer you a token of our esteem by giving you a small present. Please accept this purse of money.
SHEMIAKA	Are you offering me a bribe?
CH BROTHER	Good heavens, no! Perish the thought! It's just a gift.
SHEMIAKA	Oh, well, in that case I can't accept it. Bribes are all right. All judges accept bribes. But if I accepted a gift from you, people might accuse me of being corrupt.
CH BROTHER	Oh. – Well, actually it *is* a bribe.
SHEMIAKA	Oh, that's different then. *(He takes the purse.)* Thank you very much. – Well, if there's no further business for the court, I declare this session closed and we'll adjourn for something to eat.
OLD WOMAN	You can't close the court yet, your Honour. You've got to declare it open first.

SHEMIAKA   Oh, yes . . .

OLD WOMAN   And then you've got to judge the cases these good people are bringing before you.

SHEMIAKA   Judge cases! Of course! I knew there was something I'd forgotten. Right then. *(He sits in his chair.)* I declare this court open. What's the first case?

RICH BROTHER   It's a perfectly simple case, your Honour. *(Pointing to Poor Brother)* This man mutilated my horse.

WOOD-CUTTER } *(Together)* He killed our baby!
       WIFE }

WIDOW   He murdered my husband!

SHEMIAKA   Murder! Mutilation! Killing babies! – *(To Poor Brother)* I'm forming a very unfavourable impression of your character.

POOR BROTHER   I didn't mean to do it.

SHEMIAKA   And as if that wasn't bad enough, you've come to court all tied-up with bits of rope! You look ridiculous. Where's your sense of respect?

POOR BROTHER   Sorry.

SHEMIAKA   Obviously a hardened criminal. I wouldn't be surprised if he turned out to be one of these idiots who've been causing so much trouble.

(Enter the Officer.)

OFFICER   Your Honour, we've found one!

SHEMIAKA   You've found one what?

OFFICER   An idiot. The biggest idiot you ever saw in your life.

SHEMIAKA Really?

OFFICER He's outside. Shall I bring him in?

SHEMIAKA At once! I was getting bored with this case, anyway. I'll soon put a stop to this nonsense.

OFFICER Guards! Bring in the prisoner!

(The Rich Brother, Poor Brother, Wood-Cutter and his Wife, and the Merchant's Widow retire, and sit down.)

(The Idiot is marched in by several Guards.)

IDIOT Hello.

SHEMIAKA Are you an idiot?

IDIOT I don't know.

OFFICER He is, your Honour. Just wait till you hear what he was doing.

SHEMIAKA What were you doing?

IDIOT I was digging a well.

SHEMIAKA You idiot! You imbecile! How could anyone be so stupid as to dig a well?!

OFFICER Um ... no, your Honour, we haven't got to the stupid bit yet ...

SHEMIAKA Oh, sorry. Carry on.

IDIOT Well, I dug my well, and then I thought to myself, 'What am I going to do with all this earth I've dug up out of the well?' you see -

SHEMIAKA Yes ... I'm following it so far ...

IDIOT So I thought to myself, 'Can't leave it there. Big heap of earth. Looks ugly.' So I thought, 'I know what I'll do! - I'll dig a hole and bury it.'

(Pause.)

SHEMIAKA   Yes?

OFFICER   Don't you see? He dug a hole to bury the earth! So I arrested him for being an idiot.

SHEMIAKA   Sounds perfectly sensible to me. Public-spirited, in fact. We can't have great heaps of earth left lying about. It would look terrible.

OFFICER   Yes, but – Well, just let him go on.

IDIOT   Well, I dug a big hole, you see, and put all the earth in it. But then, when I turned round, there was another big heap of earth just like the one I'd just buried.

OFFICER   You see?

SHEMIAKA   Of course! – You fool! How could anyone be so stupid? – You were right, Officer, this man is an idiot. – Of course there was a heap of earth left over, you imbecile! You should have dug the hole twice as big!

(Pause.)

IDIOT   Oh, yes! I never thought of that . . .

OFFICER   Um . . . No, actually, your Honour –

SHEMIAKA   What a fool! – Take this idiot away, Officer, and make him dig a hole twice as big.

OFFICER   Yes, but –

SHEMIAKA   I know the way to deal with fools like him.

OFFICER   Yes, but –

SHEMIAKA   At once!

OFFICER   Yes, your Honour. – Guards! Remove the Prisoner.

(The Idiot is marched off by the Guards. The Officer follows.)

SHEMIAKA Good. We won't be troubled by any more stupidity. Now, where was I?

OLD WOMAN You were about to hear the evidence against this man.

SHEMIAKA Oh, yes. The mass-murderer and baby-strangler. *(To Rich Brother)* Please. Carry on.

CH BROTHER Thank you, your Honour. - This man is my brother -

SHEMIAKA What?! You're the brother of this notorious criminal? - Then I don't think we can believe a word you say.

CH BROTHER But your Honour, you've only got my word for it that he *is* a criminal.

SHEMIAKA Exactly. He might be a perfectly innocent man.

OLD WOMAN But in that case there's no reason why you shouldn't believe his brother.

SHEMIAKA That's true. - Carry on.

CH BROTHER Thank you. This man -

SHEMIAKA Wait a minute. - *(Pointing to Elena)* Who's that?

OLD WOMAN She's a visitor.

SHEMIAKA A visitor?

ELENA My name is Elena, your Honour. People call me Elena the Wise. I've come to see how you dispense justice.

SHEMIAKA By all means. I'm sure you'll find it very interesting. If there's anything you don't understand don't be afraid to ask.

ELENA   I won't.

SHEMIAKA   Good. Now where were we?

RICH BROTHER   I was telling you about my brother.

SHEMIAKA   So you were.

RICH BROTHER   Two days ago he came and asked if he could borrow my horse to bring home his fire-wood. So, out of the kindness of my heart, I lent it to him. And when he returned it - what do you think? It had no tail! He'd pulled its tail off!

SHEMIAKA   Outrageous!

RICH BROTHER   Naturally, I brought him to court to demand that he be punished and made to pay compensation.

SHEMIAKA   Naturally.

RICH BROTHER   On the way, however, we stayed the night with this wood-cutter.

WOOD-CUTTER   That's right, your Honour. We took them in for the night. And do you know how this man repaid our hospitality? *(He points to the Poor Brother.)*

SHEMIAKA   No.

WIFE   He killed our baby!

WOOD-CUTTER   Murdered him in cold blood!

WIFE   My poor little baby! What had he ever done to hurt anyone?

WOOD-CUTTER   So naturally we brought him to court to demand that he be punished and made to pay compensation.

SHEMIAKA   Naturally.

WIFE   But on our way here we crossed over a high bridge, and suddenly this man - this baby-killing monster - ran to the side and threw himself off.

SHEMIAKA   What did he do that for?

WIDOW   So that he could murder my husband. There we were, quietly minding our own business, crossing the frozen river with our sledge, when this ruffian jumped on my husband and killed him instantly.

SHEMIAKA   Appalling!

WIDOW   What a terrible way to die! Crushed to death!

SHEMIAKA   Absolutely!

WIDOW   So naturally I brought him to court to demand that he be punished and made to pay compensation.

SHEMIAKA   Naturally. - This is an extremely serious case. I shall need some time to consider my verdict, so I'll hear another case while I'm thinking about it. *(Calling)* Officer!

(The Officer enters.)

OFFICER   Yes, your Honour.

SHEMIAKA   Send in the next case.

OFFICER   Yes, your Honour. *(Calling)* Send in the next case!

SHEMIAKA   How are you getting on with that hole, by the way?

OFFICER   It's finished.

SHEMIAKA   So you've got rid of all the earth?

OFFICER   Well, no. There's still a big heap left over.

SHEMIAKA   What?

OFFICER	Well, there would be . . .
SHEMIAKA	Fools! I thought I told you to dig it twice as deep.
OFFICER	We did!
SHEMIAKA	Well, you obviously didn't dig it deep enough. Go away and dig a deeper one.
OFFICER	Yes, but –
SHEMIAKA	At once!
OFFICER	Yes, your Honour.

(The Officer goes off. Meanwhile the Priest, the Farmer's Wife, the Doctor and the Priest's Maid-Servant have entered.)

(The Rich Brother, the Poor Brother, the Wood-Cutter and his Wife, and the Merchant's Widow retire and sit down.)

SHEMIAKA	I'm surrounded by idiots! The fools can't even bury a heap of earth! It's lucky some of us have our wits about us. – Now. What's this next case about?
FARMER'S WIFE	It's about my calf, your Honour.
PRIEST	No, it's about *my* calf, your Honour.
SHEMIAKA	Make your minds up.
FARMER'S WIFE	That's just it, your Honour. The calf belongs to my red cow, yet this priest claims it belongs to him.
PRIEST	It is mine!
FARMER'S WIFE	You see? – How can it be his?
PRIEST	It is mine, your Honour.

SHEMIAKA	How do you know?
PRIEST	It must be.
SHEMIAKA	Why?
PRIEST	Because I gave birth to it.
	(Pause.)
SHEMIAKA	I see . . . Well, that does put a rather different complexion on the matter . . .
RMER'S WIFE	But, your Honour - it's ridiculous! How can he give birth to a calf? He's a man, not a cow!
SHEMIAKA	Yes, now you come to mention it, it does seem a bit odd. - How did you come to give birth to a calf?
PRIEST	It's a miracle!
SHEMIAKA	I see. That would explain it then.
PRIEST	The other day, just after supper, I was struck down with a terrible stomach-ache, and my belly began to swell till it was as tight as a drum. I sent my maid-servant here to run to the doctor, and his diagnosis was that I was pregnant.
SHEMIAKA	Is the doctor in court?
DOCTOR	Yes, your Honour. That's perfectly correct. I diagnosed that the patient was pregnant and would soon give birth to a calf.
PRIEST	Well, when I heard this I didn't know what to do. I rushed out of doors and ran into the night like a man possessed. At last I found shelter in a barn and fell asleep. Next morning, when I awoke, the pains in my stomach were gone, and lying next to me on the straw was a little calf - my child! And then this woman came along and tried to take it away from me.

FARMER'S WIFE   It's my calf! How could he give birth to it? It's all a pack of lies!

SHEMIAKA   You can't ignore the medical evidence.

FARMER'S WIFE   It's a conspiracy! They're in it together! They're trying to steal my calf that I was going to fatten up for our Christmas dinner.

PRIEST   She's going to eat my baby!

SHEMIAKA   This is a very difficult case. I'll have to think about it and come back to it later. - *(Calling)* Officer! Bring in the next case.

(The Officer enters with a Woman who lent money and a Man who borrowed money. The man walks with the help of a stick.)

(Meanwhile the Priest, Farmer's Wife, Doctor and Maid-Servant retire and sit down.)

OFFICER   Here they are, your Honour.

SHEMIAKA   Have you finished that hole yet?

OFFICER   Well . . . It's very deep

SHEMIAKA   But is it deep enough to bury all the earth?

OFFICER   Well, no, because -

SHEMIAKA   Then it's not finished, is it?

OFFICER   But, your Honour -

SHEMIAKA   Call all your men together and don't stop digging till it's deep enough.

OFFICER   Yes, but -

SHEMIAKA   At once!

OFFICER   Yes, your Honour.

(The Officer goes off.)

SHEMIAKA Really! Pretending it was finished when it wasn't! He must think I'm stupid or something. - What's the next case about?

WOMAN It's about an unpaid debt, your Honour. One year ago this man came to me and asked if he could borrow ten gold pieces, promising to repay them within six months. Since he's well-known in town as a very religious man I trusted him and lent him the money. But now he refuses to give it back.

SHEMIAKA *(To the Man)* Is this true?

MAN Your Honour, it's true that I borrowed the money. I needed it because I hurt my leg and couldn't work for a time. As you see, I still have to walk with a stick. But when the six months were up I repaid the loan. She seems to have forgotten about it, but I'm prepared to swear on oath that I've given the money back.

WOMAN Very well. I know him to be a pious and religious man. He wouldn't dare tell a lie on oath. Let him swear.

SHEMIAKA An excellent idea! He can swear an oath on the Bible. - We used to have a Bible round here somewhere. What's happened to it?

OLD WOMAN It's propping up the leg of your chair.

SHEMIAKA So it is. *(He removes the Bible from under the leg of his chair and gives it to the Man.)* Here you are. Swear on that.

MAN With pleasure. *(To Woman)* Could you hold that for a moment, please. I need both hands. *(He gives the Woman his stick to hold, then takes the Bible in one hand and holds up the other to swear.)* I swear upon the Holy Bible that I have given this woman her money back, although she doesn't appear to realise it.

WOMAN   Well, if he swears it then I suppose I must believe him. I must have forgotten about it somehow. - *(To Man)* I apologise.

MAN   Not at all. Could I have my stick back?

WOMAN   Of course. *(She gives his stick back to him.)*

SHEMIAKA   Right then. I'll give judgement on all three cases at once. **(He sits on his chair, which without the Bible to support it is now lop-sided.)** What's the matter with my chair? It wasn't like this a minute ago. Someone's been interfering with it!

OLD WOMAN   No, your Honour -

SHEMIAKA   I can't give judgement on a wobbly chair! It would be an insult to the dignity of the law. Court is adjourned until I can get it mended.

OLD WOMAN   But what are all these people supposed to do in the meantime?

SHEMIAKA   I don't know. There must be something. - I've got it! They can all go and help dig that hole.

VARIOUS VOICES   What?!

SHEMIAKA   *(To the Old Woman)* Show them where to find the shovels. - That way. Come along. Don't dawdle.

(Reluctantly everybody goes off, except for Shemiaka and Elena the Wise. Shemiaka examines the leg of his chair.)

I don't understand it. It was perfectly all right a minute ago, but now three of the legs seem to have grown longer.

(Elena picks up the Bible which the Man left behind and gives it to Shemiaka.)

ELENA   Try this.

(Shemiaka replaces the Bible under the leg of his chair.)

SHEMIAKA   Amazing! *(Sitting on it)* It's as good as new! Excellent! What did you say your name was again?

ELENA   People call me Elena the Wise.

SHEMIAKA   Well, you certainly know how to mend chairs. I remember hearing a story once about someone called Elena the Wise. She used to go around helping people with her wisdom. It can't have been you though, because she only visited stupid people.

ELENA   One finds stupidity everywhere. Even the best of us are stupid at times.

SHEMIAKA   Yes. Shocking, isn't it? And the worst of it is these idiots never *realise* how stupid they are. Even if you tell them they don't believe you.

ELENA   Telling them is just a waste of time.

SHEMIAKA   Exactly. Look at the fools I have to deal with. People just don't realise how difficult it is being a judge. For a start, none of the people who come to my court ever seem to agree about anything.

ELENA   If they agreed there'd be no need for a judge to decide the matter.

SHEMIAKA   But if they don't agree how on earth do they expect me to know? I mean, take these cases I've been hearing today. How am I supposed to know what to do? Wood-cutters giving birth to horses and pulling their tails off, priests jumping on to babies from bridges, and the rest of it. - Most people couldn't even remember it all without getting confused.

ELENA   I see what you mean.

SHEMIAKA   What's it got to do with me, anyway?

ELENA   You're the Judge. They come to you for justice.

SHEMIAKA   Justice . . . Yes, I think I've heard of it . . . But how can I give them that?

ELENA   Well, first of all, you shouldn't take bribes.

SHEMIAKA   Shouldn't I? But all judges take bribes. I thought it was part of the job.

ELENA   No. You should decide a case on the facts. If you take a bribe it might influence your decision.

SHEMIAKA   Oh, that's all right. I always forget which side gave it to me.

ELENA   Next, you have to find the truth.

SHEMIAKA   The truth? What's that?

ELENA   It can often be hard to find.

SHEMIAKA   Then how am I ever going to decide these cases?

ELENA   Let's take them one by one. First there's the man who pulled the tail off the horse and killed the baby and that woman's husband.

SHEMIAKA   Obviously a dangerous lunatic.

ELENA   But you haven't heard his side of the story.

SHEMIAKA   How could you believe anything a criminal like that said? I'll sentence him to be hanged. And after that I'll sentence him to life-imprisonment, and then a further ten years' hard labour for the horse's tail.

ELENA   But then how are you going to compensate the injured parties?

SHEMIAKA   That's a point. This case is too difficult. Let's go on to the next one.

ELENA   That's the priest who says he gave birth to the calf.

SHEMIAKA   That's easy. The doctor agrees with him, so it's two against one.

ELENA   You don't think it sounds a bit unlikely?

SHEMIAKA   I must admit I did at first. But nobody could make up a story like that. The farmer's wife must be lying.

ELENA   Perhaps they're both telling the truth.

SHEMIAKA   Is that possible? I thought it had to be either one or the other.

ELENA   Not necessarily.

SHEMIAKA   This is even more complicated than I thought. - What's the last case?

ELENA   The man who borrowed the money and swears he returned it.

SHEMIAKA   Now this case *is* easy. He's a very religious man. He wouldn't tell a lie on oath. Even the woman who lent him the money admits that.

ELENA   No, he didn't tell a lie on oath. But he hasn't given the woman her money back all the same.

SHEMIAKA   But how can that be?

ELENA   Didn't you see? - Call them back and I'll show you.

SHEMIAKA   All right. *(Calling)* You can all come back now.

(Enter the Old Woman, the Man who borrowed money, the Woman who lent money, the Farmer's Wife, the Priest, the Doctor, the Maid-Servant, the Merchant's Widow, the Wood-Cutter and his Wife, the Rich Brother and the Poor Brother. They are all slightly dishevelled.)

RICH BROTHER   About time too!

PRIEST   Expecting us to dig holes! It's disgraceful!

MAN   And me with my bad leg too!

WOOD-CUTTER   It's outrageous!

POOR BROTHER   I was quite enjoying it. At least they had to untie me.

SHEMIAKA   Quiet! It's time to decide the cases.

ELENA   We'll begin with the unpaid debt.

WOMAN   But it's all right. I believe him now.

ELENA   All the same I'd like to see him swear again. - *(To Shemiaka)* Give him the Bible.

SHEMIAKA   Bible?

OLD WOMAN   Under your chair.

SHEMIAKA   Oh yes . . . *(He gives the Man the Bible.)*

ELENA   Now swear.

MAN   Certainly. *(To Woman, giving her his stick.)* Would you mind holding that again? – Right. I swear I've given this woman her money back. All right? Satisfied?

ELENA   Perfectly. I believe you.

MAN   Good. Then if I can have my stick back I'll be on my way.

ELENA   Not so fast. – *(To Woman)* Give me that stick.

WOMAN   Here you are.

(Elena takes the stick and breaks it in half.)

ELENA   Here is your money. The stick is hollow and your money's inside. – He told the truth when he said he'd given it back, but he's still a liar and a cheat. *(She gives the Woman the stick.)* Take your money and go in peace. *(To Man)* And as for you, you're fined a hundred roubles for trying to deceive the court. Now go, before I make it two hundred.

(The Woman and the Man go off.)

SHEMIAKA Amazing! I'd never have worked that out on my own. There's more to being a judge than I realised. Let's go on to the next case. Where's the priest and the farmer's wife?

PRIEST }
RMER'S WIFE }   *(Together)* Here, your Honour.

SHEMIAKA Right. Who's got the stick? I'll soon settle this.

PRIEST   Neither of us has got a stick, your Honour.

SHEMIAKA What? – Then how am I supposed to decide?

ELENA   I'd like to question the doctor.

DOCTOR	Of course.
ELENA	You diagnosed that this man was pregnant and would shortly give birth to a calf?
DOCTOR	That is correct.
ELENA	Didn't this strike you as at all odd?
DOCTOR	A scientist has to keep an open mind.
ELENA	What evidence did you base your diagnosis on?
DOCTOR	An examination of the patient's water.
SHEMIAKA	His water?
DOCTOR	That's right.
SHEMIAKA	Has he got a well on his property?
OLD WOMAN	No, your Honour - *(She whispers in his ear.)*
SHEMIAKA	Oh, his water! - I see. Carry on.
ELENA	Did you visit the patient personally to examine him?
DOCTOR	That wasn't necessary. His maid-servant brought a specimen of his water to me.
ELENA	I see. Then I'd like to question the maid-servant.
MAID-SERVANT	Yes?
ELENA	Is what the doctor says true?
MAID-SERVANT	I should say so! The things they expect you to do! I mean, I don't mind carrying the eggs home from market or doing the laundry, but there are limits. I mean, it's not nice, is it? Suppose I were to meet some young men from the town, like that handsome soldier who's staying at the inn for example, and he said, 'What's that you've got in that bottle?' - What could I say?

ELENA   But you performed the errand?

AID-SERVANT   Of course. I always do what I'm told.

ELENA   And nothing happened on the way?

AID-SERVANT   Nothing at all.

ELENA   You didn't fall over, for example?

AID-SERVANT   Well, yes, I did fall over.

ELENA   But you didn't spill what you were carrying?

AID-SERVANT   Well, yes, I did. But, as luck would have it, there was a cow in a field nearby making water –

SHEMIAKA   Making water?

AID-SERVANT   That's right.

SHEMIAKA   I thought cows made milk.

OLD WOMAN   No, your Honour – *(She whispers in his ear.)*

SHEMIAKA   Oh, making water! – I see. Carry on.

AID-SERVANT   So I filled up my bottle and took it to the doctor. Though what he wanted it for I can't imagine.

ELENA   Thank you. I think that explains the doctor's diagnosis.

PRIEST   But what about my pains and my swollen belly? How do you explain that?

ELENA   What did you have for supper that night?

PRIEST   Stew.

ELENA   And what was in the stew?

PRIEST   I don't know. My maid-servant cooked it.

AID-SERVANT   Beans, cabbage, onions, garlic, radishes, lentils, green peppers and spice.

PRIEST   It was delicious. I had three helpings.

ELENA   Then I shall give judgement. The calf's mother is
           the red cow belonging to the farmer's wife. - *(To
           Farmer's Wife)* You may take your calf and go. -
           The court advises the priest to eat less, the maid-
           servant to look where she's going, and the doctor
           to combine science with a little common-sense. -
           Next case!

           **(The Priest, Doctor, Maid-Servant and the Farmer's
           Wife go off.)**

SHEMIAKA   Incredible! I'd never have managed to get to the
           bottom of that on my own. I've never seen
           judging like it! And I should know.

RICH BROTHER   Thank heavens we've got a judge with a bit of
               intelligence for a change.

SHEMIAKA   For a change?

RICH BROTHER   *(After a slight pause)* I mean instead of all the
               idiots one meets in other judges' courts, your
               Honour.

SHEMIAKA   Oh - quite.

RICH BROTHER   As you've already heard, this is a very simple
               case. This man has committed three monstrous
               crimes, and the court has only to decide how to
               punish him sufficiently severely, and how to
               compensate us for our losses.

SHEMIAKA   Absolutely. Well, I've got a couple of ideas about
           punishing him, but the compensation is a tricky
           matter.

ELENA   First I'd like to hear the accused give his side of
           the story.

SHEMIAKA	Why not? It's a bit unorthodox, but you seem to know what you're doing.
ELENA	*(To Poor Brother)* Tell us what happened in your own words.
OR BROTHER	I'd cut some fire-wood in the forest, but I didn't know how I was going to get it home. I am a poor man, but my brother is rich, so I went to him and asked if I could borrow his horse. Very kindly he agreed.
CH BROTHER	You notice that even he has to admit how kind I was?
ELENA	The court takes note.
OR BROTHER	So the next morning I went to collect the horse, but when I asked for a bridle and harness for it my brother refused.
CH BROTHER	The agreement was to borrow the horse. Nothing was said about a harness.
OR BROTHER	What good was a horse to me without a harness?
CH BROTHER	Exactly! That was the whole point of the joke! - But my brother has no sense of humour.
OR BROTHER	I had to get my wood home. I loaded it on to my sledge, but how was I to attach it to the horse? The only thing I could think of was to tie it to the horse's tail. It worked for a while, but then the sledge got caught on a tree-root, and the horse pulled and strained, and then suddenly his tail came off.
CH BROTHER	You notice he doesn't attempt to deny it?
OR BROTHER	I was very sorry. Now the poor horse won't be able to flick the flies away when they bother him -

RICH BROTHER	Never mind the horse – what about me?! I demand compensation!
ELENA	What happened next?
POOR BROTHER	On the way to court we stayed the night with this wood-cutter and his wife.
WOOD-CUTTER	That's right. We were kind and took him in.
POOR BROTHER	All evening they feasted and made merry with my brother, while I sat in the corner without so much as a crust. When it was time to sleep, they made up the beds on top of the stove for warmth. My place was right on the very edge.
WOOD-CUTTER	We shouldn't have let him on the stove at all.
WIFE	We should have let him sleep on the cold floor.
POOR BROTHER	All night long they pushed and shoved and said 'Move over', and I did my best, but suddenly I fell off the edge. I landed on the cradle and the baby was killed.
WOOD-CUTTER	You see? He admits it!
WIFE	My poor baby! He killed him!
POOR BROTHER	I was very sorry, but what could I do? – So the next day, as we journeyed to court, I thought to myself, 'The Judge will certainly find me guilty, and I'll be hanged, for I'm a poor man and have nothing to bribe him with. Why shouldn't I end it all now?' We were crossing a high bridge at the time so I ran to the side and threw myself off, to put an end to my misery. But, as luck would have it, the merchant and his wife were crossing on the frozen river below, and the merchant broke my fall.
WIDOW	He killed him!
POOR BROTHER	I didn't mean to.

WIDOW	Murdered him in cold blood! I demand that he be punished and made to pay compensation.
SHEMIAKA	No punishment could be too severe for such a monster!
ELENA	But then there is the question of compensation. You all demand compensation, do you not?
H BROTHER	Certainly!
OD-CUTTER	A baby's worth substantial damages!
WIDOW	A husband's worth even more!
ELENA	Then I'll give judgement. - *(To Poor Brother)* I sentence you to keep your brother's horse until it grows a new tail. Then you must give it back.
H BROTHER	What? But that will never happen!
ELENA	Secondly, I sentence you to take the wood-cutter's wife and keep her until she has another baby. Then you can repay him for the one he's lost.
OD-CUTTER	What? I'm not letting him have my wife! We can have another baby without his help.
ELENA	And thirdly, I sentence you to go and stand on the ice exactly where the merchant stood, and let his widow jump on you.
WIDOW	What? But it's a thousand to one chance that I'll hit him! I'll be smashed to bits!
H BROTHER	*(To Shemiaka)* Your Honour, these judgements are ridiculous!
OD-CUTTER	Outrageous!
WIDOW	Idiotic!

SHEMIAKA   They seem very sensible to me. It's exactly what I'd have done myself.

POOR BROTHER   Well, give me the horse and the wood-cutter's wife, and I'll go and stand under the bridge.

RICH BROTHER   No. It's all right. I'm prepared to let the whole matter drop.

WOOD-CUTTER   Yes, so am I. Let's say no more about it.

WIDOW   I'm not jumping off that bridge.

POOR BROTHER   But we must carry out the judgement of the court.

RICH BROTHER   Listen. Give me my horse back and I'll give you fifty roubles.

WOOD-CUTTER   Let me keep my wife and I'll give you a hundred.

WIDOW   Two hundred, if only I don't have to jump off that bridge!

POOR BROTHER   All right.

ELENA   Then that's settled. Pay him his money and go on your way.

(**The Rich Brother, the Wood-Cutter and his Wife, the Merchant's Widow and the Poor Brother go off.**)

SHEMIAKA   Well, that's that. I think we can congratulate ourselves on a good morning's work. Now we can adjourn for something to eat.

ELENA   And I must be on my way.

OLD WOMAN   You're going?

ELENA   I must. I'm needed in so many places.

OLD WOMAN   But how are we going to get along without you?

SHEMIAKA   The same as we always did, of course.

OLD WOMAN   That's what I'm afraid of.

SHEMIAKA   What are you talking about? - This young lady has been most helpful, but don't forget that I would have given exactly the same judgement myself in the last case. What I don't understand is why they all complained about it . . .

ELENA   There's nothing more I can do. I must go. Goodbye.

(Elena goes off.)

OLD WOMAN   She's right, of course. There are some things even she can't do anything about.

SHEMIAKA   Absolutely. It all goes to prove what I've always said. Everything is exactly as it should be.

(Enter the Officer of the Court.)

OFFICER   Your Honour, about this hole -

SHEMIAKA   Ah, there you are. It's time for my dinner. All this judging has given me an appetite.

OFFICER   Your dinner's ready. But about this hole -

SHEMIAKA   Excellent! I'll go and eat it then.

OFFICER   Yes, your Honour.

(Shemiaka goes off.)

Oh, by the way, your Honour, be careful you don't fall down the -

SHEMIAKA   *(Off-stage)* Aaaaah!

(A thud. Silence. The Officer rushes off and returns immediately.)

OLD WOMAN   Is he all right?

OFFICER   Yes. He was lucky. He fell on his head.

The Cyclops
A story from Greece

CHARACTERS

SILENUS
CHORUS of satyrs, (both sexes, numbering 6–12)
ODYSSEUS
SAILORS (non-speaking)
THE CYCLOPS

NOTE: The Chorus's lines may be distributed
between groups or individuals as desired. However,
for convenience in an unrehearsed reading of the
play I suggest that the Chorus is restricted to six
voices, and I have numbered the speeches
accordingly. In a rehearsed performance, of course,
these suggestions need not be adhered to, and more
complex voice-patterns may be aimed for.

In front of the Cyclops' cave.

(Enter Silenus.)

SILENUS   I hate goats. – And I don't like sheep much either.
Yet here I am, on this rocky island in the middle of
nowhere, looking after sheep and goats. – Me!
Silenus! The great Silenus, cup-bearer to the god
Dionysus, treated like a common herdsman. The
trouble is, my master, Dionysus, the god of wine, has
vanished off the face of the earth. Yes – the god who
gave mankind the greatest of all gifts, wine, has
disappeared. So naturally I set out with all my sons

and daughters to find him. But we were ship-
wrecked on this rocky coast where rumbling Etna
belches smoke and flame, and captured by the
Cyclops. And if you don't know what a Cyclops is,
you can count yourself lucky. They're huge, ugly,
savage brutes with only one eye in the middle of
their foreheads. They're quite uncivilised. They live
on cheese and mutton, and they drink – can you
believe it – water! They've never heard of wine! How
uncivilised can you get? And one of them –
Polyphemus by name – has made us his slaves, to
herd his sheep and tend his stinking goats. What
sort of life is that for one who has danced with
Dionysus? – But here come my sons and daughters,
driving home the herd.

(Enter the Chorus, miming herding sheep.)

CHORUS 1	Come along you stubborn ram!
	Move yourself you lazy ewe!
2	Here is grass for you to eat.
3	Can't you hear your young ones bleat?
4	Come and feed your thirsty lambs
	Or I'll beat you black and blue.
5	No! Not that way! Come back here!
6	Stop them! Drive them to the fold.
1	Of all the beasts a man could keep
	There's nothing worse than goats and sheep.
2	Always running far and near
	Never doing what they're told.
3	Come along you stubborn ram!
	Move yourself you lazy ewe!
4	Here is grass for you to eat.
5	Can't you hear your young ones bleat?
6	Come and feed your thirsty lambs
	Or I'll beat you black and blue.

SILENUS   I never thought I'd live to see the day when the children of Silenus, the pride of the satyr race, would be forced to herd sheep and drink nothing but water. Why has Dionysus deserted us?

CHORUS: ALL   O, Dionysus, god of wine, where are you?

1   When will we hear again the mountains echo
To the sound of clashing cymbals and the piping flute?

2   Where have you gone with your dancing followers?

3   In what woods do they stamp their feet
And toss their shining hair, wreathed with vine-leaves,
Singing your praises, inspired by wine?

4   Glorious wine, bringer of laughter and song!

5   Wine, that turns sorrows into joys,

6   Wine, that makes cowards brave and the weak strong,

1   All-powerful wine, inspirer of pleasure and of love,

2   Immortal wine, that makes a man a god,

ALL   Wonderful, precious, sweet, intoxicating wine!

SILENUS   Ah, if we had some wine we might forget
The heavy labours under which we sweat
To serve this godless, one-eyed monster.
Oh, what I'd do for wine!
I'd even herd the Cyclops' sheep,
And clean his loathsome cave, and sweep
The dung up off the floor,
And cook his meals, and do whatever more
He asked of me, if in the evening
I could drink good wine, and sit and watch
The firelight flicker and the shadows leap,
And talk about old times, drink to old friends,
And fall at last into a drunken dreamless sleep.
But those days are gone.
The Cyclops will be home soon. We must go and milk the ewes.

CHORUS: 1   But wait! Look over there. There's a ship drawn up on the shore.

2   Yes, and a party of sailors have disembarked. Who can they be?

3   No visitors come to the island where the Cyclops lives, unless they're mad or lost.

SILENUS   They're carrying bags and water-flasks. They must have stopped to pick up supplies.

CHORUS: 4   Don't they know the Cyclops is a man-eating monster who likes nothing better than to feast upon his visitors?

5   They'll find their welcome in the Cyclops' jaws.

6   Quiet! Here they come.

(Enter Odysseus, followed by a party of sailors.)

ODYSSEUS   Greetings, strangers. Can you direct us to a running stream where we may fill our water-flasks? – But what's this I see? Have we come to the country of Dionysus? Unless I'm much mistaken you belong to the satyr race, the goat-footed children of Silenus.

SILENUS   I'll thank you not to mention goats to me. I'm Silenus, as you guessed, and we are satyrs. But though we may have horns and tails, our feet are nothing like a goat's. We may not be men, but we're not beasts either. But who are you, and what are you doing here?

ODYSSEUS   We are Greeks. My name is Odysseus, King of Ithaca.

SILENUS   I've heard of you.

ODYSSEUS   We come from the war at Troy.

SILENUS   So you were involved in that affair, were you? A bad business. Ten years of war, and many thousands slain, all for the sake of one unfaithful wife. And did you get Helen back again?

ODYSSEUS   We sacked the city, and restored her to her husband. Our honour was satisfied.

SILENUS   I'm glad to hear it. But what are you doing here?

ODYSSEUS   Storms drove us off course and scattered our ships. What is this place? Are you the only inhabitants?

SILENUS   These are the slopes of Mount Etna, in Sicily.

ODYSSEUS   Are there no towns or villages on the island?

SILENUS   No men live here.

ODYSSEUS   Just you and the wild beasts?

SILENUS   The monsters of the Cyclops race, the sons of Poseidon the god of the sea, inhabit the isle. They don't build towns. They live in caves.

ODYSSEUS   Who is their king?

SILENUS   They haven't got one. There's no government at all. They're utter savages.

ODYSSEUS   How do they live?

SILENUS   They neither farm the land nor follow trades. They keep goats and sheep, and live on cheese and mutton.

ODYSSEUS   They sound a gentle people. Are they kind to strangers?

SILENUS   Not really. They think strangers make an excellent meal.

ODYSSEUS   What? You mean they feed on human flesh?

SILENUS   Man-meat, they say, is tenderest of all.

ODYSSEUS *(Looking around anxiously)* Where is this Cyclops? Is he near?

SILENUS He's gone out hunting, but he'll soon be back. He'll be very pleased to see you.

ODYSSEUS I'm sure he will. But I don't think we'll wait for him. We're in a hurry. If you could let us have some food and water –

SILENUS Well, I don't know about that. We haven't any food to spare –

ODYSSEUS We wouldn't want to be forced to use violence –

SILENUS Apart from meat, of course.

ODYSSEUS An excellent cure for hunger.

SILENUS And there's milk and cheese –

ODYSSEUS Splendid. We'll pay you well.

SILENUS What use is money in this savage land? There's no buying and selling here. What else have you got?

ODYSSEUS Well, we've got some wine –

SILENUS Wine?! – Wine, you said? Did I hear right? You did say wine?

ODYSSEUS I thought you might find that acceptable.

SILENUS Where is this wine?

ODYSSEUS *(Holding up a wine-skin)* Here, in this wine-skin.

SILENUS That? There's not enough in that to wet my lips.

ODYSSEUS Of course, if you don't want it –

SILENUS Did I say that? Quick – pass it over here.

ODYSSEUS First get us food and water.

SILENUS   Yes, at once! - But wait - I'm feeling rather faint. A mouthful of wine would revive me -

ODYSSEUS   First get the food.

SILENUS   I'm on my way - Only I seem to have something stuck in my throat. Perhaps I'd better drink a little wine . . .

ODYSSEUS   Well, just a mouthful. Here you are.

SILENUS   *(After drinking)*
　　　　　Ah, what a blissful taste! It runs through every vein
　　　　　And makes me tingle from my head down to my toes.
　　　　　For wine like this I'd rob that one-eyed brute
　　　　　Of everything he owns. He doesn't frighten me.
　　　　　When I get drunk there's nothing I can't do -
　　　　　I'll walk through fire, I'll swim the widest sea,
　　　　　I'll fight an army, and I'll beat them too -
　　　　　But first I'll go and get that food for you.
　　　　　(Silenus goes off.)

CHORUS: 1   So, King Odysseus, you fought at Troy.

ODYSSEUS   Yes, and fought nobly. I killed many men in open fight, and with my cunning, famed through many lands, I brought us victory in the greatest war the Greeks have ever fought.

CHORUS: 2   It was the silliest affair I've ever heard of. Why go to war just because that woman, Helen, went off with another man? It happens all the time.
　　　　3   Are you so short of women in Greece that you have to go to war each time you lose one?

ODYSSEUS   It was a matter of honour.

CHORUS: 4   Is honour worth the lives of all those men and the destruction of a city?

ODYSSEUS   You don't understand. Justice demanded that the Trojans should be punished.

CHORUS: 5   It seems a strange kind of justice.
6   How can it be just to kill so many people?

ODYSSEUS   What do you know about it? Satyrs like you can't be expected to appreciate such things as honour and justice. You're only interested in eating and drinking. Civilised men like us have nobler aims in life, and high ideals to live up to.

(Enter Silenus with the food.)

SILENUS   Well, here's the food.

ODYSSEUS   At last! I'm starving. Quickly - give it here.

SILENUS   But wait! Look over there! The Cyclops is coming! Look out!

(The sailors run about the stage in panic, while the satyrs get in their way.)

ODYSSEUS   Quick! We must hide! Don't panic! Come on, run! This way! - No, that way! - No, the other way! - We're trapped! We're done for! - But wait a minute. Stop! *(The sailors freeze.)* Is this the way Odysseus should behave? Can a man like me, who fought ten thousand Trojans, turn and run away? Never! I'd disgrace the honour of my fellow Greeks if I was such a coward.

SILENUS   He's coming!

ODYSSEUS   But, on second thoughts, the wisest thing to do is run and hide. Quick! Into the cave!

(Odysseus and the sailors run into the cave. Enter the Cyclops.)

CYCLOPS   What are you doing standing here? Have you milked my ewes? Are the goats penned up for the night? Are the new-born lambs nuzzling their mothers, drinking their sweet milk? Have you made the cheese and churned the butter? Is my dinner ready?

SILENUS   Yes, everything's in order. Why don't you go for a nice stroll before supper?

CYCLOPS   I don't want to. I'm hungry. Where's my dinner? In the cave?

SILENUS   No, no! Don't go in there!

CYCLOPS   Why not?

SILENUS   Come over here and admire the view.

CYCLOPS   What's the matter with you? - *(Noticing the food which Silenus brought)* What's this food doing here?

SILENUS   What food?

CYCLOPS   That food!

SILENUS   I can't see anything.

CYCLOPS   Of course you can! - That food. What's it doing here? Have you been trying to rob me? - Answer, or I'll smash your skull.

SILENUS   Oh, *that* food! - Well, it wasn't me. My sons and daughters must have done it.

CHORUS: 1   No, we didn't!
        2   It was him!
        3   We saw him do it!

CYCLOPS   I'll beat his brains out!

SILENUS   No! I've just remembered. - I was protecting it from thieves. Some sailors came to rob you, but I wouldn't let them.

CYCLOPS Sailors?

SILENUS Greeks from the war at Troy. They said that they'd steal everything you own, but I stood up to them. I fought them single-handed and wouldn't let them take a thing. You wouldn't believe the trouble I go to on your behalf.

CYCLOPS How dare they? Where have they gone?

SILENUS I told them you'd be angry, but they said they didn't care, and called you - please forgive me for repeating it - an ugly, savage brute. They said they'd like to cut your ugly throat - their words, not mine - and flay your hide, and squeeze your guts out through your single eye, and do all sorts of nasty things which I'll refrain from mentioning. I told them you'd be cross.

CYCLOPS Where are they? - Light the fire. I'll slaughter them and eat them up at once.

SILENUS Using my cunning, I managed to get them all into your cave. They can't escape.

CYCLOPS *(Calling)* You there! Come out. I'm going to eat you.

(Odysseus and the sailors enter from the cave.)

ODYSSEUS Your servant is lying. He gave us the food in exchange for wine. Which is only right, for the gods command we should be kind to strangers. We had no wish to rob you. He sold us your goods.

SILENUS I swear by all the gods I never touched them. And if I'm lying then let my dear children, whom I love more than anything in the world, die for it.

CHORUS: 4 Us? Why should we die for it?

       5 He gave your goods to the strangers. We saw him do it.

       6 And if we're lying, let our father die for it.

CYCLOPS   Quiet! You're all lying. But it doesn't matter.
Whether the strangers are guilty or not I'm going to
eat them anyway. It's months since I had a decent
meal of human flesh.

ODYSSEUS   O mighty Cyclops, listen to what I say.
We came in peace, as friends.
We are not thieves, but honourable men.
They say that you're Poseidon's son,
Offspring of the mighty sea-god. Back at home in
    Greece
We have built many temples in his honour.
Will you repay us by sacrificing us to your greed?
All men honour strangers and protect them,
For hospitality is the first duty of a civilised man,
And every god will be offended if you kill us.
Too many Greeks are dead already,
Slain at the siege of Troy.
Too many widows weep and orphans mourn
In the cities of war-weary Greece.
Don't add to their number by killing us.
Learn the ways of merciful humanity
And forget your ungodly lust for human flesh.

SILENUS   If you ask me, Cyclops, when you eat him up you
shouldn't forget his tongue. If it's half as sweet as
the words it speaks it ought to be a treat.

CYCLOPS   The only god I serve is my belly.
What do I care for all the temples you've built my
    father?
Do they do me any good? If I offend the gods
By eating you, what difference will it make?
If the gods send storms and thunder,
Why, then I'll sit in my snug cave and feast
On roasted meat and cheese, and warm myself
Before a roaring fire. What more has life to offer?
If the gods are angry I don't care.

The earth will still grow grass to feed my flocks.
The only law I follow is to please myself.
Call me uncivilised - so long as my belly's full
I'm happy. Laws, custom, justice, mercy,
They only complicate existence. All I want
Is to enjoy myself, and feed on your
Sweet, tender, juicy flesh. Into the cave!

ODYSSEUS Then I've escaped the bitter pains of war
And all the dangers of the cruel sea
Merely to perish on this friendless shore.
Oh, save me, gods! If gods exist, save me!

CYCLOPS Stop talking! Into the cave!

(**Odysseus and the sailors are driven into the cave. The
Cyclops follows them.**)

SILENUS What happened to that wine?

CHORUS: 1 He took it into the cave with him.

SILENUS A pity. I could do with some. Well, it's too late now.
I'm not going in there while he's eating those men.
It makes me feel quite ill to think about it.

CHORUS: 2 If a Cyclops invites you to dinner
'No, thank you' should be your reply.

3 For the food he likes best
Is a nice roasted guest
Or a big slice of visitor-pie.

4 When a Cyclops invites you to dinner
You'd be better off staying at home.

5 You'll appreciate when you
Find you're on the menu
It's safer to dine on your own.

6 To feast upon those you invite
Is not, as a rule, thought polite.

1   But when a Cyclops has people for dinner
He gorges himself like a hog.
2   Then he sits and digests
His deceased dinner-guests,
And throws out the bones for his dog.

(Odysseus runs out of the cave.)

ODYSSEUS   Oh, horror! How can I describe what I have seen?

CHORUS: 3   What's up, Odysseus? Did you see the Cyclops eating your friends? Tell us all about it.

ODYSSEUS   He picked up two of them and felt them to see if they were fat.

CHORUS: 4   How horrible! What happened next?

ODYSSEUS   He lit a fire and put a cauldron on to boil, and prepared the sharp spits and the pans to catch the blood. Then he took one of the men and smashed his brains out on a rock, and cut him up and put him on to roast. Then, with a knife, he slit the other's throat, catching his blood in the dripping-pans, and boiled him in the pot. The rest of us cowered in terror in a corner of the cave, while he gorged himself on our friends. At last he gave a loathsome belch, and leaned back satisfied. Then the gods inspired me with a wonderful idea. I poured a cup of wine and gave it to him saying 'Drink this wine, O Cyclops, and enjoy the gift of Dionysus.' He drained it at a gulp and seemed to find it good, so I poured another. Soon he was getting drunk and started to sing, while in the corner my companions moaned and sobbed with fear. I seized my opportunity and slipped away.

SILENUS   You mean you've let that godless monster have your wine? What a waste! A savage like that doesn't know how to appreciate it.

ODYSSEUS	I've got a plan, but I'll need your help.
SILENUS	If there's fighting involved you can count us out.
ODYSSEUS	Don't you want to escape your slavery here and go back to your drunken revels with Dionysus? Who wouldn't prefer to dance through the forests with the god of wine than to dwell on these bare rocks with goats and sheep? I offer you freedom and revenge!
CHORUS: 5	Freedom!
6	Revenge!
1	What are you going to do?
2	What sort of revenge? Are *you* going to eat *him?*
ODYSSEUS	My plan's a clever one. I'll give him some more wine -
SILENUS	But there'll be nothing left for us!
ODYSSEUS	When you escape you can have all the wine you want.
SILENUS	Yes, but I want it now.
ODYSSEUS	We'll get him drunk, and soon he'll fall asleep.
SILENUS	Then will we run away?
ODYSSEUS	No. First he must be punished for his savage greed. I've found a wooden stake inside the cave. One end of it I'll sharpen to a point and put it in the fire until it's hot. Then when the point is glowing red I'll pull it out and thrust it deep into the Cyclops' single eye, burning his eye-ball out and blinding him.
CHORUS: 3	Wonderful!
4	Splendid!
SILENUS	An excellent plan! I can see this savage brute's no match for a civilised man like you.

ODYSSEUS   Then we can all leave on my ship and we'll be free!

CHORUS: 5   You can count on me!
     6   I'll help you, Odysseus.
     1   Yes, and me!

ODYSSEUS   Then be quiet, and obey my orders. First we must get him drunk.

SILENUS   Perhaps we'd better taste the wine to make sure it's strong enough.

CHORUS: 2   A good idea! I'll do that for you.
     3   Yes, so will I! We'll need a second opinion.

ODYSSEUS   Leave it alone! We'll need every drop we've got. - Now be quiet. He's coming.

(The Cyclops enters from the cave. He is drunk.)

CYCLOPS   What are you doing out here? Where's that wine? I want more wine.

ODYSSEUS   Here it is. There's plenty left.

CYCLOPS   *(Drinking)* I've never known drink like it. What did you say that god was called whose spirit is in wine?

ODYSSEUS   Dionysus.

CYCLOPS   What sort of god is he?

ODYSSEUS   Giver of heaven's best gifts to humankind.

CYCLOPS   I drank him and he tasted very good. But why does he live inside a skin?

ODYSSEUS   That is his temple. He doesn't mind where he lives.

CYCLOPS   I don't like the skin, but I like what's inside.

ODYSSEUS   Then drink some more.

CYCLOPS   I know what I'll do. I'll invite my brother Cyclops to join me in a drink.

ODYSSEUS   No, don't do that.

CYCLOPS   Why not? I want to share it with my friends.

ODYSSEUS   If you share it there'll be less for you.

CYCLOPS   But I feel happy and I want to see my friends. It would be more fun to drink with others.

ODYSSEUS   But they'll take all the wine, and leave you with nothing.

CYCLOPS   That's true. What should I do?

SILENUS   Stay here, and drink more wine.

CYCLOPS   Perhaps I should. And anyway my legs feel rather funny. I think it would be nice to sit down. *(He sits down suddenly.)* This seems a pleasant spot.

(Silenus takes the wine-skin and cup from Odysseus, and sits next to the Cyclops.)

SILENUS   Here, Cyclops, let me pour you out some more.

CYCLOPS   Go ahead.

SILENUS   I'll just taste it to make sure it's all right.

CYCLOPS   Give it here. Put it in the middle where I can see it. - You, stranger, what's your name?

ODYSSEUS   My name is Nobody.

CYCLOPS   Well, Nobody, you're my friend. To thank you for this wine I'm going to give you a reward.

ODYSSEUS   What's that?

CYCLOPS   I won't eat you until I've eaten every one of your companions. I'll save you to the last.

ODYSSEUS   You're very kind.

CYCLOPS   Don't mention it. - *(To Silenus, who has drunk the cup of wine)* But where's that wine gone?

SILENUS   I don't know.

CYCLOPS   You drank it, thief! Do you think I'm blind? Pour out some more.

SILENUS   At once. Just see how rich it shines within the cup. Then lift it to your nose - like this - and smell the tempting fragrance. Then drink it down - like this -

CYCLOPS   You've done it again! Give me the cup. Nobody will pour my wine for me. - Come here, Nobody. Pour my wine.

(Odysseus sits beside him and pours the wine.)

ODYSSEUS   Here you are then. Drink it down.

CYCLOPS   *(Drinking)* Wonderful! What a god this wine must be!

ODYSSEUS   Then have some more.

CYCLOPS   *(Drinking)*
             Delicious! What a glorious feeling!
             I can't stand up, my head is reeling!
             One minute the earth's beneath my feet
             The next it's whirling in the sky!
             My friends - you're all my friends - I want to say
             How much I like you all - my dear old friends.
             And best of all, my dear friend Nobody.
             I like you very much. I won't let anybody
             Hurt you till it's time for you to be eaten.
             I even like this greedy satyr here.
             Silenus, you're my friend.

SILENUS   Whatever you say.

CYCLOPS   I like you so much that I want to kiss you.

SILENUS   What?!

CYCLOPS   Come here.

SILENUS   No thanks!

CYCLOPS   I just want to be friendly.

SILENUS   Not with me!

CYCLOPS   Then be like that. I'm feeling sleepy. I think I'll go
and have a lie-down.

(The Cyclops stumbles off into his cave.)

ODYSSEUS   The moment's come! He's drunk. Now we'll prepare
the red-hot stake to thrust into his eye. Are you
ready?

CHORUS: 4   Lead the way.
5   We'll follow you.
6   Our courage can't be shaken.

ODYSSEUS   O god of fire, come to my aid!
Help me to burn away the monster's eye.
O god of sleep, seal up his sight
Until I've brought him to eternal night.
Stand by us now, O gods,
Or else I'll never worship you again.

(Odysseus goes off into the cave.)

CHORUS: 1   The time has come.
2   It's too late to retreat.
3   Revenge is ours, and our revenge is sweet.
4   The stake's prepared.
5   The Cyclops is asleep.
6   We'll teach him that he can't make us herd sheep.
1   We'll get our own back with a clever trick,
And win our freedom with a pointed stick.

2   I'll hold the stake!
3   I'll thrust it in his eye!
4   I'll twist it round and make the monster cry.
5   He'll scream and kick and blindly punch the air -
6   Unless, of course, there's someone standing there.
1   Yes, that's a point.
2   This could be dangerous.
3   He'll strike out blindly and he might hit us.

4   I wish we had some wine to make us brave.
5   But since we haven't how should we behave?
6   Like satyrs always do. Let's run away.
1   Yes, that's the best idea I've heard all day.

(Odysseus re-enters from the cave.)

ODYSSEUS   What's all this noise? Are you trying to wake him up? - What are you hanging around out here for? We've got work to do.

SILENUS   We're ready. What do you want us to do?

ODYSSEUS   Come in the cave and help me burn the monster's eye.

SILENUS   Say no more. My children here are all eager to help.

CHORUS: 1   Try and stop us! - Unfortunately, though, I seem to have got a cramp in my leg.
2   I've got something in my eye!
3   How strange. Just now, while I was standing here, I sprained my ankle.

ODYSSEUS   Sprained it standing still?

CHORUS: 3   I said it was strange.

ODYSSEUS   What about you?

CHORUS: 4   How very odd. Exactly the same thing's just happened to me.

5 And I've just remembered - I've got to go and meet someone.

6 That's right. It's me. We won't be long -

ODYSSEUS Cowards! Don't you want to escape from this monster?

SILENUS Of course we do. But as you pointed out, we're cowards. That's the problem.

ODYSSEUS Aren't you ashamed?

SILENUS Of course not. We're satyrs - what do you expect? We're all of us the way we are because the gods decreed it so. If the gods had wanted us to be brave, they wouldn't have made us so cowardly. As it is, who are we to interfere with their wishes?

ODYSSEUS Very well. I'll do it on my own. There are some men among my crew that I can trust to back me up. - As for you, as soon as you hear the monster yell, drive his sheep down to the shore and put them on the ship. We'll take them with us and have fresh meat on our voyage. - Do you think you can manage that?

SILENUS Stealing's no problem. That comes naturally. Rely on us.

ODYSSEUS Then let's to work, and do a deed that will be famous through the ages, for as long as tales are told.

(Odysseus goes into the cave.)

CHORUS: 1 The sleeping Cyclops snores within his cave
Dreaming a drunkard's dreams.

2 The stupid brute believes that we're his friends
And trusts us, but he'll quickly learn
What sort of friends we are.

3 Now let the red-hot spike approach his eye.

4   Now drive it home, deep in the socket.
5   See the blood spurt, and hear his eye-ball
     Sizzle as it burns away his sight.
6   See how the noble Greeks repay
     This monster for his savage ways!

(From within the cave the Cyclops screams.)

CYCLOPS   Aaah! I am murdered! Help me! Save me friends!

CHORUS: 1   What's wrong?

CYCLOPS   I'm blinded!

CHORUS: 2   What, with drink you mean?

CYCLOPS   Nobody's hurting me!

CHORUS: 3   Then there's nothing wrong.

CYCLOPS   Nobody's blinded me!

CHORUS: 4   Then you're not blind. Why make a fuss if nobody has hurt you?

CYCLOPS   Where's Nobody? Don't let him get away! Where's Nobody?

CHORUS: 5   Nobody's nowhere. Where else could he be?

CYCLOPS   You know who I mean. The stranger who gave me wine.

CHORUS: 6   You should be careful. Wine is dangerous stuff.

(The Cyclops enters from the cave, blind, and stands blocking the entrance.)

CYCLOPS   I've got them trapped inside my cave. They can't escape. I'll have my revenge. I'll kill them as they leave.

SILENUS   *(To Chorus)* Quick, now's our chance to steal his sheep. Come on!

(Silenus and the Chorus go off.)

CYCLOPS   *(Sitting in the entrance to his cave)*
Is there no-one to pity me?
Will no-one help me, blinded by this cruel stranger,
Helpless and alone? - Where are my sheep?
My flocks of goats and sheep, whose woolly backs
My hands have stroked so many times,
Whose udders I have squeezed to get the warm,
    sweet milk,
Have you deserted me? Why can't I hear you
    bleat?
Are you grieving for your master's eye
That cruel Nobody has blinded?
But I will be revenged. They won't escape.
And when I lay my hands upon that stranger
Who deceived me with his treacherous wine,
I'll smash his skull and strew his brains upon the
    ground,
And then perhaps my sorrow and my pain will be
    relieved.

(Silenus and the Chorus re-enter.)

SILENUS   What's the matter, Cyclops? You don't look very well. Is something wrong?

CYCLOPS   Where are the strangers? I'll make sure they don't escape.

SILENUS   You're too late. Look. They're over there.

CYCLOPS   Where?

SILENUS   There. In front of you. Can't you see?

CYCLOPS   I'm blind.

SILENUS   Don't worry. I'll direct you to them. To your right.

(The Cyclops rises and stumbles blindly about the stage, while Odysseus and the sailors creep out of the cave.)

CYCLOPS   This way?

SILENUS   That's right. A little to the left. You've got them!

CYCLOPS   Where? - Ow! Now I've banged my head.

SILENUS   The other way! Quick! They're escaping!

CYCLOPS   What? This way?

SILENUS   That's it.

CYCLOPS   I'll get them! - Ow! I've stubbed my toe.

SILENUS   Don't stop! You've nearly caught them!

CYCLOPS   *(Tripping up)* Now I've fallen over. Where have they gone?

SILENUS   They're over there!

CYCLOPS   Which way? I can't see anything! Which way?

ODYSSEUS   Here I am, Cyclops, safe and sound, Odysseus, King of Ithaca.

CYCLOPS   What's that? Odysseus - I recognise your voice. You're Nobody. What's this new name of yours?

ODYSSEUS   Odysseus. The name my father gave me. Now you see how those who feed upon human flesh are punished.

CYCLOPS   Then the oracle is fulfilled that prophesied that I would lose my eye to someone called Odysseus, coming from Troy. I thought that it would be a giant, mighty and powerful, who would come against me, but you, a miserable and feeble man, have conquered me with wine and blinded me.

ODYSSEUS   It's no more than you deserve.

CYCLOPS But yet the oracle foretold that you would not escape punishment. It is decreed that you will wander far and wide across the stormy seas and never find your family or your home till ten long years have passed and you've become a stranger in your own land.

ODYSSEUS What do I care for your oracles? What's done is done. Now we'll leave you to your savage ways and return to Greece.

(Odysseus and the sailors go off.)

SILENUS Goodbye, Cyclops. We're taking your sheep with us, and we'll think of you each time we slaughter one.

CYCLOPS No, not my sheep! What will I live on?

SILENUS You should have thought of that before.

CYCLOPS I'll be revenged! You won't escape! I'll kill you all! *(Stumbling around blindly)* Where are you?

CHORUS: 1 Over here!

CYCLOPS *(Moving towards the voice)* Where?

CHORUS: 2 *(From the other side of the stage)* Behind you!

CYCLOPS Here?

CHORUS: 3 No, over here.

CYCLOPS You're making fun of me.

(The satyrs dance around the Cyclops, keeping just out of reach.)

CHORUS: 4 You'll never catch us!
5   Just you try!
6 We're free!
1   We're on our way!
2 And now we'll laugh and dance and sing
    To celebrate this day.

3	We'll leave this brute to shout and curse.
4	And moan and wail and weep.
5	With any luck he'll starve to death
	Without his precious sheep.

SILENUS   A savage monster such as him
Will always get a beating
When he takes on a clever man,
For men are best at cheating.

CYCLOPS   I'll be revenged! I'll get you yet!
Where are you? Come back here!

CHORUS: 6   You must be joking!
1   Not a chance!
2   It's time to disappear.
3   Our days of slavery are past.
4   The monster's going to miss us.
ALL   Now all we'll do is drink good wine
And dance with Dionysus!

**(And, so saying, Silenus and the Chorus dance around
the stage and off, while the Cyclops stumbles off in the
wrong direction.)**

NOTES

These plays are intended to work with a minimum of scenery and props,
and may be performed with none at all in the classroom or drama-studio.
But they also lend themselves to more elaborate production, and will
benefit from imaginative costuming, lighting, mime and movement, and
in some cases music. Always, though, the speaking of the words is the
important thing, and simplicity should remain the key-note.

My stage-directions are fairly basic, and leave much to the producer's
discretion. They may easily be adapted to different circumstances and
stages. Casting can also be flexible, particularly with regard to sex, which
can often be disregarded for casting purposes. Cases where this would be
inappropriate are sufficiently obvious, and will in any case depend upon
the style of a particular production.

The Lost Ring

The story of Shakuntala comes from India's national epic, the
Mahabharata (*Mahabharata Book I, The Book of the Beginning*,
translated and edited by J. A. B. van Biutenen, University of Chicago
Press 1973). This story formed the basis of what is generally considered
the masterpiece of India's greatest poet, Kalidasa, whose play on the
subject probably dates from the end of the fourth century A.D. (There is a
translation by Michael Coulson in *Three Sanskrit Plays*, Penguin 1981.)
The motif of the lost ring is Kalidasa's addition, but it is found in
numerous other stories from all over the world. (There is an English
example called 'The Fish and the Ring' in *English Fairy Tales* by Joseph
Jacobs, first published 1890, The Bodley Head 1968.)

I have followed Kalidasa in the main outlines of the plot, but with a
considerable degree of freedom and change of emphasis. The main
additions to the plot involve the introduction of Saradvata to provide a
stronger motivation for the curse, the expansion of the roles of Madhava,
Shakuntala's friends and the servant-girl, Shakuntala's denunciation of
the King when she is rejected (which is closer to the version in the
Mahabharata), and the reduction of the King to beggary at the end.

Much of the dialogue is written in a rather formal mode, and this should
be reflected in the style of acting and in the production as a whole.

The Stupid Judge

The motif of the stupid judge is, I suppose, common in folk and other
literature, but I am unable to point to any specific source. It serves as a
framework for free adaptations of several tales, not all of them Russian.

The story of the poor brother comes from 'Shemiaka the Judge' (though the original the judge is corrupt rather than stupid). Both this and 'The Pregnant Priest' are from Alexander Afanasiev's great collection of Russian folk tales. The figure of the wise maiden is also from Russian tradition, though not from any particular tale. The story of the loan exist in many versions, but is probably best known in Europe as one of the cases judged by Sancho Panza in his capacity as governor of his island (*Don Quixote* II xlv). And the joke about the hole to bury the earth has probably been told by virtually all peoples, in all times.

The Cyclops

The Ancient Greek satyr play—of which 'The Cyclops' of Euripides is the only complete example to come down to us—was intended to be performe as an afterpiece to a trilogy of tragedies, and treated the mythological stories in a spirit of irreverent comedy.

There are several translations of Euripides' play, including one by Shelley and more recently by William Arrowsmith (in *Euripides II, The Complete Greek Tragedies*, edited by David Grene and Richmond Lattimore, University of Chicago Press 1956), and by Roger Lancelyn Green (in *Two Satyr Plays*, Penguin 1957).

Euripides took the story, of course, from the ninth book of the Odyssey, and—apart from introducing Silenus and the satyrs, and omitting such incidents as the escape by means of the sheep which would be difficult to stage—he followed his source quite closely. I have followed Euripides with similar fidelity, and some of the dialogue is close to being free paraphrase of the original, though other parts, particularly the choruses, I have treated more freely, and in one instance—the Cyclops' lament near the end—I have followed Homer instead of Euripides.

In production the play will be enhanced by music and dance during the choral interludes (which may be sung), and the use of masks might well be effective, particularly for the Cyclops, who could perhaps have a second one for when he has lost his eye. His gigantic size, however, is probably best left to the audience's imagination.